PRIMER contents

Independent
Churches
**Working
Together**

Primer is produced by the Fellowship of
Independent Evangelical Churches (FIEC);
a family of Independent churches working
together to reach Britain for Christ. Find out
more at *fiec.org.uk*

Eschatology – the study of the 'last things' – is very often the last thing we want to talk about.

For many of us it conjures nightmarish scenes of the antichrist and lakes of fire; for others it's the equally nightmarish scene of Christians speculating over pre- or post-millennial schemes and the timing of the rapture.

Even away from those debates, eschatology struggles to find a place. Most systematic theologies manage to cover almost all of their major topics (the doctrines of God, creation, salvation, the church, etc.) without a mention of eschatology. And then, just as the end is nigh, a final, often brief chapter – a kind of postscript – setting out what the future holds.

And yet, while *Primer* is still relatively young, we want to address the last things early. One of the main reasons for that is the vital role the future plays in the New Testament. Think, for example, of the evangelistic preaching in Acts. The message is that the risen Christ has been appointed the world's Lord and will return to judge. One day soon his enemies will be made his footstool (as Peter says in Acts 2 and Paul says in Acts 17). For unbelievers there is the call for repentance, for believers there is the call to patience and endurance. Indeed, Paul can characterise conversion as the turn "from idols to serve the living and true God, and to wait for his Son from heaven, whom he raised from the dead – Jesus, who rescues us from the coming wrath" (1 Thess 1:9-10). Furthermore, this is not a marginal thought: Paul returns to it in that letter and twice urges the church to "encourage one another with these words" (1 Thess 4:18, 5:11). And Paul is not alone: Peter (1 Peter 1:3-9) James (1:1-12), and the author to the Hebrews (11:1-12:3) all make the future central to their encouragement and exhortation.

A second reason for choosing eschatology is that it helps us understand the whole flow of history and our place within it. Throughout the Old Testament we look forward to *the day of the Lord*, the day when God will act to save and to judge. And yet when we turn to the New Testament we discover that there is not simply *one* day. We live between the first and second comings of Christ. As Peter announces in Acts, the death and resurrection of Christ and the pouring out of the Spirit means that we already live in the last days (Acts 2:17). Eschatology is no longer simply a matter of the future. The end is nigh and the end is now.

It is hard to overestimate how important this is. Reflecting on Paul's letters, Don Carson argues "that the unifying worldview behind these epistles is an eschatological awareness of the dawning of the age to come." Greg Beale has developed this thought at some length in his excellent book *A Biblical Theology of the New Testament*, arguing that what holds the whole NT together is a shared storyline. In outline it is that…

D.A. Carson "Reflections on Salvation and Justification in the New Testament." *Journal of the Evangelical Theological Society 40* (1997): 602-603.

> "Jesus' life, trials, death for sinners, and especially resurrection by the Spirit have launched the fulfillment of the eschatological already-not yet new-creational reign, bestowed by grace through faith and resulting in worldwide commission to the faithful to advance this new-creational reign and resulting in judgment for the unbelieving, unto the triune God's glory.

G. K. Beale, *A New Testament Biblical Theology: The Unfolding of the Old Testament in the New* (Grand Rapids: Baker Academic, 2011), 16.

This perspective opens our eyes to the need to understand the times we live in and to carefully locate ourselves between salvation accomplished and the fuller salvation to come. Our great prayer is that this issue of *Primer* will help you to do that in a way that generates worship, joy, patient endurance, and faithfulness in the present.

To that end, we begin with an article helping us to understand more of this already/not yet tension by Stephen Witmer. Next we have John Stevens outlining the various evangelical views of the future and the difference they make now.

The next two articles consider the eternal futures of humanity. Brad Green annotates a passage from Augustine's *City of God*, a remarkable passage penned over 1,500 years ago which joyfully ponders the new creation and addresses some perennial questions. Next Adrian Reynolds has read and reflected on several recent books on hell, helping us to navigate the debate and engage with it sensitively.

Two final articles are designed to help the future to shape the present life of the church. Brad Bitner tackles the significant question of continuity between this world and the world to come, and then finally Graham Beynon orientates us to the book of Revelation. It can be an intimidating book but Graham shows us how its vision of the present and the future can shape the imagination of the church and to stir her worship.

DAVID SHAW is the Editor of *Primer*. He is part-time Theological Adviser for FIEC and part-time lecturer in New Testament and Greek at Oak Hill Theological College, London. He's married to Jo and they have four children.

 @_david_shaw

AUGUSTINE OF HIPPO (A.D. 354 – A.D. 430) was the Bishop of Hippo in North Africa and a prolific preacher and writer. He was converted in A.D. 381, partly thanks to the prayers of his longsuffering mother, Monica, becoming one of the most influential figures in Christianity ever.

GRAHAM BEYNON is pastor of Grace Church, Cambridge, and also Director of Independent Ministry Training at Oak Hill College. His PhD was from St Andrews University examining the theology of Isaac Watts and he is also the author of a number of books.

BRAD BITNER teaches New Testament, Biblical Theology and Greek at Oak Hill College where he also serves as Acting Academic Dean. He is an Elder at London City Presbyterian Church.

BRADLEY G. GREEN teaches theology at Union University in Jackson, Tennessee. Amongst other things, he has written *Colin Gunton and the Failure of Augustine* and *Covenant and Commandment: Works, Obedience, and Faithfulness in the Christian Life*.

 @greenbradleyg

ADRIAN REYNOLDS is Training Director for FIEC and was previously Director of Ministry for The Proclamation Trust. He has authored several books including *Teaching Numbers* and (with his wife Celia) *And Then He Knew Her: A biblical view of sex*.

 @_adrianreynolds

JOHN STEVENS is FIEC's National Director and one of the pastors of Christchurch Market Harborough. He teaches on courses at Oak Hill Theological College, Edinburgh Theological Seminary, Union School of Theology and the Cornhill Training Course.

 @_johnstevens

STEPHEN WITMER is the pastor of Pepperell Christian Fellowship in Massachusetts. He has a PhD from Cambridge University in New Testament, teaches New Testament at Gordon-Conwell Theological Seminary, and is the author of *Eternity Changes Everything*.

 @stephenwitmer1

FUTURE PRESENT

*The already/not yet kingdom,
and why it matters*

by Stephen Witmer

A friend told me about travelling to Switzerland with
his family some years ago. At one point in the trip, they
found themselves stranded on a rainy train platform
with two hungry children and only a granola bar or
two. Time passed, tension grew, and his wife began
to reproach him for his poor planning. Then, quite
suddenly and dramatically, the clouds parted and
they saw the spectacular Swiss Alps. His kids stared in
stunned silence. His wife apologised. Peace and gladness
were restored. In some respects, nothing had changed.
But in another sense, much had. The family had been
reminded of where they were headed. The future
changed their present. Though they were still hungry,
they were happy and humbled.

The grand storyline of Scripture begins with the original creation and moves through humanity's fall to God's redemption, but it doesn't stop there. It climaxes with a future, final restoration of God's earth and God's people. Revelation 21-22 completes the canon with an extended vision of the new creation and its citizens. The penultimate verse of the entire Bible contains Jesus' promise, "Yes, I am coming quickly," together with the eager response of his people, "Amen! Come, Lord Jesus!" The Bible thus ends on tiptoe, yearning for God's future.

It's worth pondering the fact that God chose to reveal to us something of this final future. He needn't have done that. He could have planned it all and then said nothing of it. It seems clear that he intends our (admittedly imperfect) knowledge of our future to affect our living in the present. He means for there to be a connection between eschatology (when we live, and where we're headed) and ethics (how we live). Christians have understood this from the earliest days of the church. Eschatological themes appear in the Christian letters, homilies, and apologetic works of the first several centuries, often connected to pastoral exhortation.

The story of the rainy train platform and the Swiss Alps raises an important question. Is the eschatological message of the Bible essentially, 'The end is almost here, therefore live now in light of that imminent reality?' Or do Jesus and the apostles go further than that? Do they claim that, in some sense, the end has in fact already arrived? We might ask this question using the kingdom language of Jesus and the New Testament gospels. Is the kingdom of which Jesus speaks a future reality? A present reality? Somehow both? This question has received starkly differing answers in New Testament scholarship over the past 200 years. To better understand the main issues at stake, and (more importantly) to gain deeper insight into the eschatological teaching of Jesus and the New Testament, it's helpful to review briefly the course of the debate. We'll then be in a better position to understand the already/not yet kingdom Jesus brings, as well as why it matters so much for life.

HOW DOES THE KINGDOM COME?

The 18th century **Enlightenment** raised fundamental questions about the proper source of authority, as well as the supernatural worldview of the New Testament. It also heightened confidence in human potential for achieving progress, and promoted the idea of a utopian future that was its own, secularised version of Christian eschatological hope. This Enlightenment utopian future, however, arose from the historical process itself and from innate human potential, rather than arriving as a gracious action of God. In light of the intellectual ferment created by the Enlightenment, New Testament scholars began to grapple with basic questions about the Bible and the kingdom of God. Was it possible or necessary, in an enlightened world, to understand the kingdom in Jesus' teaching as a future, external, supernatural work of God? Might the kingdom be understood in more naturalistic, internal terms? Could humans achieve the kingdom through their own efforts? For our purposes, we might categorise some of the main approaches to the kingdom in the past 200 years as 'the present kingdom,' 'no kingdom,' and 'the future kingdom.' As we'll see, each of these are alternatives to *inaugurated eschatology*: the biblical teaching that Jesus, at his first coming, brought the kingdom of God truly but not yet fully.

The present kingdom

Nineteenth century scholars such as Albrecht Ritschl and Adolf von Harnack taught that the kingdom of God in Jesus' teaching was a present, ethical reality; a human task rather than a divine gift. They acknowledged that Jesus adopted the idea of a future, visible, external rule of God from his Jewish contemporaries. But this was the husk rather than the kernel of Jesus' thought and teaching. The real core was the kingdom as a present, inner, ethical reality, focusing on universal truths like the fatherhood of God and the importance of love. This liberal view 'de-eschatologised' Jesus' teaching, essentially reducing eschatology to ethics. We shouldn't expect Christ to bring the kingdom in an external, historical, future sense. Rather, the kingdom arrives as we learn to love one another. "The kingdom comes by coming to the individual, by entering into his soul and laying hold of it... everything that is dramatic in the external and historical sense has vanished; and gone, too, are all the external hopes for the future."

Adolf Harnack, *What Is Christianity?* (New York: Putnam's Sons, 1908), 60–61.

This liberal view correctly perceived a present aspect of the kingdom in Jesus' teaching (e.g. Luke 11:20). However, it ultimately proved unconvincing to many. Making the teaching of the New Testament more palatable to modern sensibilities required a serious distortion of the biblical text, as the supernatural kingdom was reinterpreted to refer to something humans achieve for themselves. In at least some of Jesus' teachings, the kingdom is clearly a divinely-wrought, future reality that involves surprising reversals, rather than merely continuations, of the present order (Luke 13:27-30). There is also a clear apocalyptic strain in Jesus' teaching that cannot be domesticated into a merely internal ethic (e.g. Matthew 24:36-44; 25:31-46). Moreover, the liberal view failed to explain basic and important historical questions, such as why Jesus' contemporaries would want to kill him for teaching the importance of love. Thus, at the beginning of the 20th century, the liberal view was severely critiqued from multiple directions.

Apocalyptic = end-of-the-world events involving final judgment or destruction.

No kingdom

The 19th century approach to the kingdom had accepted that Jesus did in fact teach about the kingdom, but had reinterpreted the kingdom as a human achievement. A more radical approach emerged in the early 20th century in the work of the German scholar William Wrede. Wrede's Jesus was a non-apocalyptic Galilean prophet, and his eschatological teaching recorded in the gospels was in fact not his, but a later addition. Wrede famously argued that the 'Messianic Secret' in the Gospel of Mark was the invention of the early church, designed to explain why the historical Jesus never actually claimed to be the Messiah. What's known as Wrede's *thoroughgoing scepticism* thus radically called into question the reliability of the New Testament gospels themselves.

Non-eschatological understandings of Jesus have persisted in more recent times through the influence of scholars such as John Dominic Crossan, Burton Mack, and the Jesus Seminar (an academic study group established in the 1980s). According to such readings, Jesus was a wandering sage. These approaches, like

Wrede's, are highly sceptical of the historical authenticity of the New Testament gospels. The Jesus Seminar famously voted with coloured beads on which New Testament sayings of Jesus were authentic, concluding that only a very few (not the eschatological ones) were definitely authentic. Both Wrede and his more recent heirs-apparent have received sustained criticism for their non-eschatological readings of Jesus, the thoroughgoing scepticism that undergirds it, and (in some cases, such as the Jesus Seminar) their dubious methodology. Additionally, the radically sceptical approach appears unnecessary if Jesus can be understood within the Jewish milieu of his own day. This was in fact the approach of the starkly different, and massively influential, work of Albert Schweitzer.

The future kingdom

At the beginning of the twentieth century, Albert Schweitzer mounted a massive challenge to the 19th century liberal approach to Jesus and the kingdom in his books *The Mystery of the Kingdom of God* and *The Quest of the Historical Jesus*. Schweitzer's view, known as 'consistent eschatology,' interpreted Jesus as a thoroughly eschatological figure, one who believed the kingdom of God was wholly future and supernatural. In fact, Schweitzer argued that Jesus mistakenly expected the future coming of the kingdom in his own lifetime. Jesus went to his death in Jerusalem precisely to force this coming of the kingdom, but failed to do so.

Schweitzer's work was a major advance on the 19th century, 'present kingdom' approach because of his demonstration that Jesus was an eschatological figure who believed in a future, public coming of the kingdom. However, Schweitzer's view that Jesus erroneously thought the kingdom was *imminently* future generated a key irony at the heart of his work. Although Schweitzer argued convincingly against liberal scholarship that, in fact, eschatology was at the core of Jesus' self-understanding and teaching, nonetheless, when it came to *applying* Jesus' teaching to modern life, Schweitzer advocated a position very similar to liberal scholarship. Jesus' outmoded and incorrect eschatology had to be discarded (after all, the kingdom did not come in his day as he thought it would), and his teaching of love, or 'reverence for life,' preserved. Schweitzer's views live on in our day. Bart Ehrman, in his 1999 book *Jesus: Apocalyptic Prophet of the New Millennium*, argues that Jesus mistakenly believed the world would end in his lifetime, but that Jesus' ethical views can nonetheless 'probably' produce a better society in our day.

But neither Schweitzer nor Ehrman provide a convincing case for their claim that Jesus believed the full, final kingdom of God would come in his own day. Schweitzer pointed to passages such as Matthew 10:23: "When you are persecuted in one place, flee to another. Truly I tell you, you will not finish going through the towns of Israel before the Son of Man comes." But this passage is better understood as referring to the continuing mission to Israel, which lasts until Jesus' second coming. And other *imminence* passages are better understood to refer more immediately to events such as Jesus' transfiguration (e.g. Mark 9:1 and 9:2-8). Moreover, in Jesus' teaching, eschatology and ethics are so closely linked that the attempts of Schweitzer and his modern heirs to reject the former while preserving the latter are unconvincing.

HOW DOES THE PRESENT/FUTURE KINGDOM COME?

As we've just seen, attempts to reinterpret Jesus' kingdom teaching as a wholly present reality (e.g. the 19th century liberal view), to remove his kingdom teaching altogether (Wrede, the Jesus Seminar), or to understand the kingdom as a wholly future reality (e.g. Schweitzer, Ehrman) are all inadequate in important ways. In each, the kingdom of God, understood as God's supernatural gift, provided at a future point in history, disappears. It is either reinterpreted as a present human achievement; removed from the teaching of Jesus altogether; or relegated to a mistaken belief of the historical Jesus which cannot seriously be believed by his modern followers. Moreover, crucially for our purposes, in each of these cases, the close connection between eschatology and ethics, which is so prominent in Jesus' teaching and the rest of the New Testament, is severed. In 19th century liberalism, eschatology effectively *becomes* ethics. In Wrede's reading, there is no eschatology to shape ethics, since the eschatology is the later addition of the church. Even in Schweitzer's work, eschatology must eventually be discarded when it comes to modern application; all that remains to carry over from Jesus' teaching is his ethic of love.

The eschatological teaching of the New Testament is more complex than any of these views recognises, and more closely integrated with ethics than any of these views allows. On the one hand, the kingdom of God is clearly a future reality. Jesus teaches that people will come from all corners of the earth to "take their places at the feast" in the future kingdom (Luke 13:29). This future aspect of the kingdom fits the many New Testament passages that describe supernatural eschatological events still to come (e.g. Mark 13; 1 Corinthians 15; 2 Thessalonians 2; Revelation 21-22). The New Testament repeatedly describes the Christian life as one of waiting for these future events. The Thessalonian Christians, "turned to God from idols to serve the living and true God, and to *wait for his Son from heaven*, whom he raised from the dead, Jesus, who rescues us from the coming wrath" (1 Thessalonians 1:9-10). The Corinthian Christians were not lacking any spiritual gift, "as you *eagerly wait* for our Lord Jesus Christ to be revealed." (1 Corinthians 1:7; cf. Galatians 5:5; Philippians 3:20; Hebrews 9:27-28; Jude 21). The native environment into which Christians are spiritually reborn is future-oriented hope (Romans 8:24).

On the other hand, another important stream of New Testament teaching emphasises the *present* arrival of the kingdom and the end-time promises of God. Jesus said, "But if I drive out demons by the finger of God, then the kingdom of God has come upon you," (Luke 11:20). This fits with Paul's claim that the ends of the ages have come upon his readers (1 Corinthians 10:11), the assertion of the writer of Hebrews that Christians are living in the last days (Hebrews 1:1-2; cf. 1 Peter 1:20-21), and the Apostle Peter's claim at Pentecost that the end-time prophecies of Joel were in fact being fulfilled in his own day (Acts 2:16-17).

> The 'last days' is a phrase used in the Old Testament to point to the end time, the eschatological age in which the prophetic writings would be fulfilled (Isaiah 2:2, Hosea 3:5, Micah 4:1, cf. Acts 2:17, 2 Tim 3:1, Hebrews 1:1-2, 2 Peter 3:3 cf. 1 Peter 1:20-21).

Importantly, Jesus' kingdom parables often simultaneously highlight both present and future aspects of the kingdom of God. The kingdom is pictured both as a tiny mustard seed (a shocking image for Jews, who understood the kingdom as God's climactic, public, end-time rule) and also as a massive tree (Matthew 13:31-32). The kingdom is like leaven hidden inside three measures of flour (again, a shockingly small and humble image) and also as a fully-leavened loaf (Matthew 13:33). In the 20th century, several scholars began to articulate an understanding of the New Testament teaching that the kingdom of God is here, but not fully; *already*, and *not yet*.

Geerhardus Vos taught at Princeton Theological Seminary from 1893-1932. In his book *The Pauline Eschatology* (1930), he developed an understanding of inaugurated eschatology in the Pauline letters. Vos presented two diagrams:

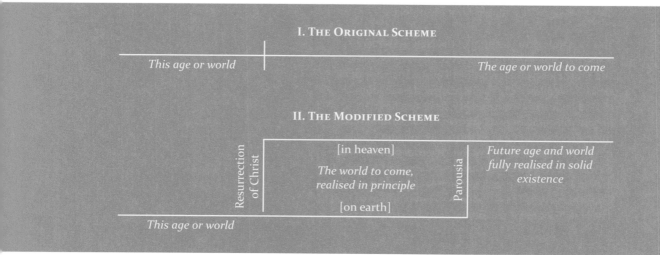

I. THE ORIGINAL SCHEME

This age or world | *The age or world to come*

II. THE MODIFIED SCHEME

Resurrection of Christ

[in heaven]
The world to come, realised in principle
[on earth]

Parousia

Future age and world fully realised in solid existence

This age or world

The first shows the traditional Jewish understanding of *this age* as distinct from *the age to come*. The second shows the Pauline understanding that the resurrection of Jesus created an overlap of the ages, in which the world to come is "realised in principle" even as the present age continues until the return of Jesus. Vos sought to understand key Pauline doctrines, such as justification and the work of the Holy Spirit, within this reconfigured eschatological framework.

The Swiss theologian Oscar Cullmann also expressed the already/not yet nature of the kingdom. In his 1946 book *Christus und die Zeit* (*Christ and Time*), Cullmann contrasted the Jewish and Christian views of history, also using two diagrams:

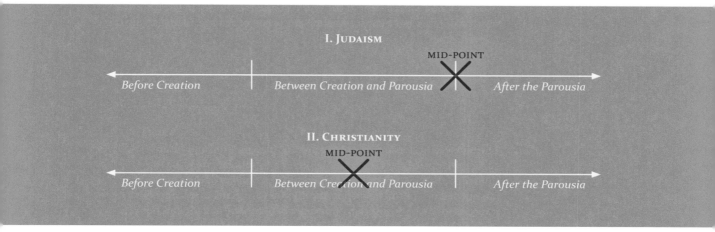

The key difference in the Christian view was that the mid-point of history was now no longer marked by the future coming of Jesus, but by his first coming. "Therefore [Jesus] sees Satan already fallen from heaven, he already expels demons 'by the finger of God,' he heals the sick, he checks the power of death, he forgives sins and explains that the Kingdom of God has already come, although he holds fast on the other hand to the future character of this Kingdom." In Cullmann's view, the tension between already and not yet was central to the New Testament. "The *new element* in the New Testament is not eschatology, but what I call the *tension* between the decisive 'already fulfilled' and the 'not yet completed,' between present and future. The whole theology of the New Testament, including Jesus' preaching, is qualified by this tension." Cullmann famously illustrated this with a war analogy: "The decisive battle in a war may already have occurred in a relatively early stage of the war, and yet the war still continues."

Oscar Cullmann, *Christ and Time* (London: SCM Press, 1951), 83.

Oscar Cullmann, *Salvation in History* (New York: Harper and Row, 1967), 172. Quoted in Hoekema, *The Bible and the Future*, 303. Emphasis original.

Cullmann, *Christ and Time*, 84.

The American New Testament scholar George Eldon Ladd articulated a similar view in his 1964 book *Jesus and the Kingdom* (later published as *The Presence of the Future*). Ladd emphasised the fundamental importance of properly defining the kingdom of God. Rejecting on the one hand a definition that made the kingdom a wholly future realm of redemption (e.g. Schweitzer) and on the other, an understanding of the kingdom as an experience of God in the human heart (e.g. the 19th century liberal view), Ladd understood the kingdom as "the reign of God, not merely in the human heart, but dynamically active in the person of Jesus and in human history." This definition made it possible "to understand how the Kingdom of God can be present and future, inward and outward, spiritual and apocalyptic." Ladd later summarised his view of the kingdom in *A Theology of the New Testament*: "The Kingdom is God's kingly rule. It has two moments: a fulfillment of the Old Testament promises in the historical mission of Jesus and a consummation at the end of the age, inaugurating the Age to Come."

George Eldon Ladd, *The Presence of the Future* (Grand Rapids: Eerdmans, 1974), 42.

ibid.

George Eldon Ladd, *A Theology of the New Testament* (Grand Rapids: Eerdmans, 1998), 58.

HOW ARE WE TO LIVE IN THE PRESENT/FUTURE KINGDOM?

The renewed understanding of the present inauguration and future consummation of the kingdom, highlighted by scholars such as Vos, Cullmann, Ladd, and Herman Ridderbos (*The Coming of the Kingdom*), has opened up fruitful new opportunities for Christians to consider what it means to live in the overlap of the ages between the already and not yet of God's kingdom. The recovery of inaugurated eschatology allows us to see and celebrate the New Testament's close link between eschatology and ethics in a way that none of the other views presented above ever could. Because it recognises a genuinely *future* eschatology – a coming, consummated kingdom that is God's achievement and gift, not our own accomplishment – eschatology can never be reduced to ethics, as it was in the 19th century. That allows for there to be a genuine interplay between eschatology (God's action in Christ) and ethics (our actions in everyday life). Because it recognises a genuinely *present* eschatology – because God's kingdom really arrived with Jesus' first coming, as God asserted his reign in the person of Jesus – we can see that Jesus' own eschatology was not mistaken, as Schweitzer argued. Therefore, we don't need to discard it, but rather can embrace and seek to live in light of it.

Inaugurated eschatology provides us with a biblically faithful account of the paradoxes and tensions of the Christian life, many of which we experience on a daily basis. The understanding of Christian living that results brings with it enormous insight, clarity, and comfort, and also calls forth much productive activity. The already/not yet kingdom simultaneously produces hopefulness and humility within Christians, allowing us to be optimistic rather than pessimistic, while remaining realistic rather than triumphalistic. It calls us to be restless for the consummation of the kingdom and simultaneously patient as we wait for it, to live with "great impatience and patient endurance." We're restless, because we've already begun to experience God's end-time blessings, and the powers of the age to come, and we naturally want more. Come, Lord Jesus! We're patient, because we're fully assured that the future kingdom will come and we'll live in it, since we're already experiencing its very real presence among us.

Hopeful

Christians who know they're living between the already and not yet can be enormously hopeful people. Because the kingdom of God is already here in part, we know that, through Christ, we are already pronounced righteous in God's sight in advance of the final judgment (Romans 8:1). We already experience the presence and power of the Holy Spirit (Romans 5:5). We already enter into a present experience of eternal life (John 5:24; 11:25-26). Our lives are hidden with Christ, who is already raised and seated in heaven at the right hand of God (Colossians 3:1-4). Jesus' past resurrection as the 'firstfruits' from the dead has guaranteed our own future resurrection (1 Corinthians 15:20-23). God's future has broken into our present, and already "our citizenship is in heaven" (Philippians 3:20). Importantly, this is not merely an individual experience. Rather, we belong to a *community* of the redeemed (the church) in this already/not yet experience. In his important work, *The Moral Vision of the New Testament*, Richard Hays has emphasised that, "The church community is God's eschatological beachhead, the place where the power of God has invaded the world," and therefore "to live faithfully in the time between the times is to walk a tightrope of moral discernment, claiming neither too much nor too little for God's transforming power within the community of faith."

Jesus has already won the decisive victory over sin, Satan, and death, and therefore we know that his future, final victory is assured. Our present experience and enjoyment of God's end-time kingdom produces solid hope (in the full, biblical sense of that word) that a final experience of the consummated kingdom will assuredly

J. Christiaan Beker, *Paul's Apocalyptic Gospel* (Philadelphia, Fortress, 1982), 120. I explore this tension between restlessness and patience in *Eternity Changes Everything* (London: The Good Book Company, 2014).

Richard Hays, *The Moral Vision of the New Testament: Community, Cross, New Creation* (New York: HarperCollins, 1996), 27. For a helpful recent work on the church as the eschatological people of God, see Benjamin L. Gladd and Matthew S. Harmon, *Making All Things New: Inaugurated Eschatology for the Life of the Church* (Grand Rapids: Baker Academic, 2016).

be ours – just as becoming engaged to be married yields a deeper assurance that the still-future marriage will certainly be entered into and enjoyed. Our robust assurance of what we don't yet have produces inner change. We can experience difficulty and not give up; we can experience pleasure and not become addicted to it. We can live free from paralysing regret over past mistakes and missed opportunities. Speaking of Christians wracked with regret, Dallas Willard writes,

Paul David Tripp, *Forever: Why You Can't Live Without It* (Grand Rapids: Zondervan, 2011), 37.

Dallas Willard, *The Divine Conspiracy* (New York: HarperOne, 1997), 376.

Much of [their] distress comes from a failure to realize that their life lies before them. That they are coming to the end of their present life, life "in the flesh," is of little significance. What is of significance is the kind of person they have become. Circumstances and other people are not in control of an individual's character or of the life that lies endlessly before us in the kingdom of God.

The enormous pastoral power of inaugurated eschatology is unleashed when we realise that our future is fully assured. What we've already been given is our guarantee of what we don't yet have. This makes us enormously hopeful and optimistic.

Humble

But we are simultaneously humbled as we realise that the kingdom is always and only God's gift, never our achievement. The secularised utopian vision of the Enlightenment promised a future that rested in human, not divine, hands. It therefore created, in the short term, pride and triumphalism, a touting of innate human abilities. In the long term, it led to profound disillusionment, as the violent and bloody 19th and 20th centuries failed to live up to the overly optimistic promises of human progress, and Enlightenment positivism was swallowed up by a postmodern epistemology of profound scepticism.

The Christian understanding of the already/not yet kingdom provides Christians the capacity to be simultaneously hopeful and humble, optimistic and realistic. Because the kingdom is not yet here in all its fullness, we aren't surprised at the present experience of suffering in this world (Romans 8:35-39). Unlike adherents of the modern prosperity gospel, we don't expect full and final healing of the mind or body in this age, and aren't dismayed when God sustains us in suffering rather than delivering us from it. We are also appropriately humble about what we can and can't know in the present age. To borrow the terminology of Kevin Vanhoozer, we seek a hermeneutics of humility and conviction, an already/not yet epistemology. We believe that,

Kevin Vanhoozer, *Is There a Meaning in This Text?* (Grand Rapids: Zondervan, 1998), 465.

in this age, we possess adequate, though not absolute, knowledge. We boldly affirm the truth claims of the gospel while recognising that, until the last day, our knowledge will remain provisional.

Helpful

Life in the inaugurated kingdom of God makes believers not only hopeful and humble, but genuinely helpful in this age. The old accusation that being heavenly minded makes one no earthly good has enjoyed a long and illustrious history. Henry David Thoreau laid the blame squarely at the feet of the founder of Christianity. "[Jesus] taught mankind but imperfectly how to live; his thoughts were all directed toward another world." Thoreau believed people too interested in obtaining eternal life in the world to come were useless in this world; they "have a singular desire to be good without being good for anything…"

Henry David Thoreau, *A Week on the Concord and Merrimack Rivers*, ed. H. Daniel Peck (New York: Penguin, 1998), 59.

But, in fact, the future/not yet aspect of the kingdom provides Christians a crucial means of critiquing and rebelling against present, unjust realities in our world, by showing us a better one. We see that the world will not always be as it now is. Theologian Jürgen Moltmann writes,

> Faith, where it develops into hope, causes not rest but unrest, not patience but impatience. It does not calm the unquiet heart, but is itself this unquiet heart in man. Those who hope in Christ can no longer put up with reality as it is, but begin to suffer under it, to contradict it. Peace with God means conflict with the world, for the goad of the promised future stabs inexorably into the flesh of every unfulfilled present. If we had before our eyes only what we see, then we should cheerfully or reluctantly reconcile ourselves with things as they happen to be.

Jürgen Moltmann, *Theology of Hope* (Minneapolis: Fortress Press, 1993), 21-22.

The not yet of the kingdom makes us restless for more and better. In the words of Trevor Hart and Richard Bauckham, "By resisting premature closure, by keeping history open to the still future coming of God, Christian eschatology sustains our outrage against innocent and meaningless suffering." This appropriate and productive sense of outrage could never be sustained by the 19th century attempt to collapse eschatology into ethics, which made the kingdom our own achievement.

Richard Bauckham and Trevor Hart, *Hope against Hope: Christian Eschatology at the Turn of the Millennium* (Grand Rapids: Eerdmans, 1999), 41.

The not yet of the kingdom also makes us productive by holding out a future promise for us that enables us to sacrifice in the present in order to serve others. D.A. Carson calls Christian leaders to focus in their ministries on the larger contexts of eschatology and doxology:

"

Transcribed by the author from a sermon by Don Carson.

We minister, we preach, we study, we give ourselves to people with eternity's values in view that Christ may be praised. And our whole heart-throb is that on the day of his unveiling, when he returns again, he will be praised amongst the people whom we have led to Christ, and we will give them to him as his honour, his due, his glory... And we cry with the church in every generation, "Even so, come Lord Jesus! Come, Lord Jesus!"... leadership is... repeatedly connected with eschatology and doxology in Scripture... leadership is never merely professional... it is rather a life lived out... in light of the eschaton, in light of the Lord's return and for the praise of his glory and the good of his church. Otherwise, the whole thing just isn't worth it.

Richard Bauckham, 'Conclusion: Emerging Issues in Eschatology in the Twenty-First Century,' in *The Oxford Handbook of Eschatology*, Ed. Jerry L. Walls. (Oxford: Oxford University Press, 2008), 680.

N.T. Wright, *Surprised by Hope* (New York: HarperOne, 2008), 208. Emphasis original.

To be truly productive in this world, we need both the not yet and the already. If we had only a future vision of all wrongs righted, all losses restored – only a vision of the eschatological future with no present inauguration – that future might seem merely pie-in-the-sky, untethered from present realities. We might be tempted to live only for the future, rather than in the present. But the already/not yet kingdom reminds us that God has already acted decisively in the world to achieve victory through Christ. As God's end-time people, we may "[anticipate] the kingdom now in appropriately modest, flexible, never-finished ways." As God's people, filled with God's Spirit, we can seek to change the present, broken world wherever and whenever we're able, since we are fully persuaded that God will one day fully restore it completely. The already/not yet kingdom reminds us that there are things for us to be doing now as we anticipate the final, glorious consummation of the kingdom. We can't bring the kingdom – only God can do that. But we can, in the words of N.T. Wright, "build *for* the kingdom."

CONCLUSION

There are many rich resources for the Christian life found in a robust understanding of the Bible's teaching of the already/not yet kingdom. The works cited in the sidenotes of this article are one means of exploring further. George Marsden once wrote of Jonathan Edwards,

George Marsden, *Jonathan Edwards: A Life* (New Haven: Yale University Press, 2003), 4-5. Emphasis original.

If the central principal of Edwards' thought was the sovereignty of God, the central practical motive *in his life and work was his conviction that nothing was more momentous personally than one's eternal relationship to God... He built his life around disciplines designed constantly to renew that eternal perspective.*

If that could be said of every Christian, Christ's church would be strengthened and the world would be changed. P

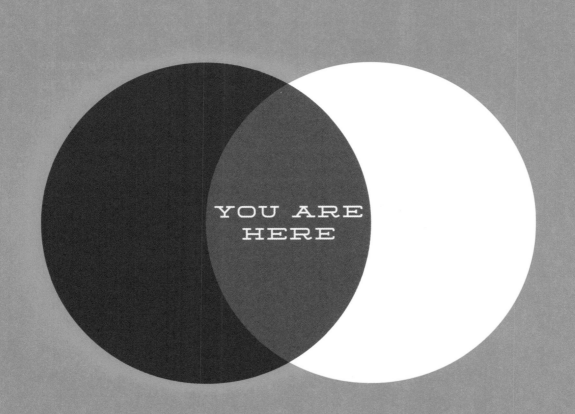

YOU ARE HERE

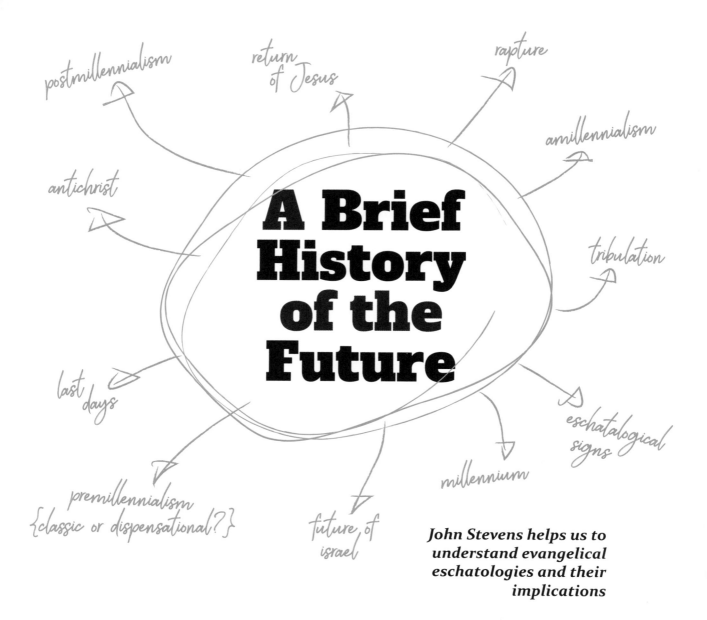

A Brief History of the Future

postmillennialism

return of Jesus

rapture

amillennialism

antichrist

tribulation

last days

eschatalogical signs

premillennialism {classic or dispensational?}

future of israel

millennium

John Stevens helps us to understand evangelical eschatologies and their implications

Eschatology is currently a neglected topic within mainstream British evangelicalism. There are a number of reasons for this. In the first place, it has been discredited by various streams of eschatological enthusiasm in the past, which have made predictions and confident assertions about world events that have proved to be inaccurate. Second, it is seen as potentially divisive amongst evangelicals who hold core gospel beliefs in common. Third, it is seen as speculative and uncertain, and therefore unprofitable. Finally it is seen as irrelevant, making little practical difference to daily Christian living or gospel mission. As the old joke puts it, many evangelicals therefore resort to some form of "pan-millennialism," meaning that they are uncertain or agnostic about the specifics but they are confident that God's purposes will "all pan out" in the end.

Popular works of prediction and fiction, such as Hal Lindsey's *The Late Great Planet Earth* and Tim LeHaye & Jerry B Jenkins' *Left Behind* novels, have similarly generated scepticism about eschatology.

However this relative neglect of eschatology is surprising in the light of the rediscovery of the fundamentally eschatological and apocalyptic character of the ministry and teaching of Jesus and the early church. As theologians such as N.T. Wright have recovered the Jewish origins of the Christian faith, they have shown both that Jesus came to fulfil the eschatological promises of the Old Testament, and that he also reworked and reinterpreted those promises around himself. Through their work, the contemporary church has been made more aware than at any time in the past that our future hope is of a renewed physical creation, the new heavens and the new earth, rather than a purely spiritual eternal state. We look forward to embodied resurrection life, which follows as "life after life after death" from an intermediate state of spiritual life with Christ when we die.

See for example, *The New Testament and the People of God* (London: SPCK 1992); *Jesus and the Victory of God* (London: SPCK,1996).

N.T. Wright, *Surprised by Hope* (London: SPCK 2007).

N.T. Wright, *The Resurrection of the Son of God* (London: SPCK, 2003), 31.

Although not articulated with as much openness as in the past, differences in eschatological convictions also underlie many of the differences in understanding the mission of the church that are prevalent amongst contemporary evangelicalism. Eschatological beliefs determine the extent to which evangelicals see their mission as one of transforming the current creation and culture, or of saving people out of this world for a future existence. Eschatological beliefs shape whether evangelicals are optimistic or pessimistic about the likely progress of the gospel in the world, and may influence their politics if they see geopolitical events, especially concerning the nation of Israel, as God's unfolding plan of salvation.

The purpose of this article is to survey in broad outline the major approaches to eschatology that have been adopted by Christians, and especially evangelicals, throughout church history, and which are likely to be encountered today. These different eschatological schemes have waxed and waned in their credibility and influence over the centuries. As will be seen, these schemes seek to systematise a wide range of biblical material, and the different conclusions they reach are often the outworking of very different approaches to biblical interpretation. It is therefore usually unfruitful simply to disagree with the details of any specific eschatological scheme, as this will not get to the root of the issue. Unity, gospel generosity, and mutual understanding are best served by appreciating the underlying theological and hermeneutical assumptions that determine the specific details.

For an in-depth analysis see especially Cornelius P. Venema, *The Promise of the Future* (Edinburgh: Banner of Truth, 2000); Donald G. Bloesch, *The Last Things: Resurrection, Judgment, Glory* (Downers Grove, Ill.: IVP, 2004).

As will be seen, there are many potential variations within the broad parameters of the major eschatological schemes, which means that people cannot always be pigeon-holed neatly into one of four positions we will soon outline. It also means that this article cannot identify and evaluate every possible variation. Instead it will need to paint with a broad brush, passing over some of the subtleties and nuances. That said, I will try to avoid unhelpful stereotypes and crass characterisations. It is inevitable that I have a bias towards the eschatological position that I find most persuasive, which I would term an *optimistic amillennialism*, but I have tried to represent other positions as accurately as I can, having drawn on the primary sources of those who advocate them.

See also Bloesch, *The Last Things*, 109-113.

The Purpose of Eschatology

The prime object of eschatology is to help us to understand how God's purposes in salvation history will unfold, from where we are now to the ultimate eternal goal of the new creation. This need arises because the crucified and risen Lord Jesus has ascended to reign at the right hand of God, and his kingdom rule has not yet been established on earth.

All evangelicals agree that we currently live in the "church age," during which the disciples of Jesus are commanded to make disciples of all nations by preaching the good news of the gospel in the power of the Holy Spirit, whom he has poured out on them.

Matt 28:16-20; Acts 1:7-8.

Rev 20:7-22:21; 1 Cor 15:20-28, 51-57; 1 Thess 5:1-11; 2 Thess 1:5-10.

All are equally agreed from Scripture that at some point in the future:

➡ *Jesus will return visibly and bodily,*

➡ *the dead will be raised and judged*

➡ *those whose names are found in the Lamb's book of life will enter into the eternal glory of the new heavens and the new earth*

➡ *those whose names are not found in this book will be condemned to an eternal judgment excluded from this new creation*

➡ *Satan will be judged and condemned and death itself will be destroyed*

➡ *Jesus will triumph over all his enemies, and will at last hand the kingdom over to his Father, with the result that all wickedness and evil will be eliminated and God will be "all in all."*

There is, therefore, general agreement about *where we are*, and *where we will end up*. This is reflected in the historic creeds and confessions of the church, and also in many evangelical statements of faith, such as the FIEC doctrinal basis, which do not adopt a detailed eschatological position. The question that eschatology presses on to ask is *how will we get there?* It seeks to identify the stages of God's unfolding plan of salvation between the present church age and the final eternal state.

The Biblical Jigsaw

The chief challenge is that there is no single passage in the Bible that provides a comprehensive and systematic explanation of how we will get from where we are to the final eternal state. Individual passages comment on disparate aspects of God's unfolding plan of salvation, and our task is to integrate these texts together to form a coherent whole. The place to start is by identifying the various component parts.

(i) The return of Jesus

Foundational to any eschatological scheme are the numerous biblical texts that speak of the future return of the Lord Jesus from heaven to earth. Whilst some have attempted to demythologise these texts, the vast majority of evangelicals agree that they teach that Jesus will return bodily and visibly from heaven to establish his kingdom on earth. The key differences concern the events (if any) that must precede this return, and the situation on earth that follows it. A further area of disagreement concerns the degree of imminence of Jesus' return. Many passages warn that Jesus' return will be unexpected, and stress the need to be ready. This might suggest that Jesus could return at any moment. Other passages, however, seem to suggest that it might be a long time before Jesus returns, and stress the need to be prepared for the long-haul of waiting and serving. The different eschatological schemes are strongly determined by whether it is thought necessary to believe that Jesus could return at any moment, or whether we should not expect Jesus to return until other identifiable events have occurred.

Matt 24:44; John 14:3; Acts 1:11; 1 Thess 4:16; Heb 9:28; James 5:8; 2 Peter 3:10; 1 John 3:2; Rev 1:7, 22:20.

See for example Matt 24:36-25:46, which interleaves parables stressing the need to be ready because Jesus will come at an unexpected time with parables that suggest the need to be ready for a lengthy wait before he returns.

(ii) The last days

The New Testament, developing and applying the language of the Old Testament prophets, speaks of a period of time that is labelled the "last days." The "last days" seem to anticipate the coming of the "last day," which will signal the end of history as we know it and usher in the eternal future. However, the precise meaning of the "last days," and when they occur, is hotly contested and influences the different eschatological schemes.

Acts 2:16-17;1 Tim 4:1-5; 2 Tim 3:1-9; 2 Pet 3:3.

Some regard the "last days" as a relatively short period of time that precedes the return of Jesus, which will be marked by a climactic escalation of human wickedness and rebellion.

For others, the "last days" describe the entire final stage of salvation history that runs from the ascension of Jesus and outpouring of the Holy Spirit to his return, and are therefore synonymous with the church age in which we currently live. On this understanding the church age will be simultaneously the period of gospel growth and church triumph, but also of persecution, suffering and rebellion against God.

Of particular relevance to eschatological schemes is the fact that both Paul and Peter seem to regard the "last days" as a present, or at least imminent, experience of the church, rather than as a period which might occur a significant time in the future. To complicate matters further, some variations of eschatological schemes may view the "last days" as a climactic time of suffering for Christians that took place in the Jewish-Roman war that culminated in the destruction of Jerusalem in A.D. 70, but which prefigures a second period of the "last days" that will come on the whole world just before Jesus returns.

(iii) The Eschatological Signs

The extended apocalyptic discourse of Jesus, which is found in **all three of the synoptic gospels**, also appears to suggest that there are a number of specific events which must occur before he returns and the final eternal kingdom is inaugurated. The following events are said to herald the "end of the age":

See Matt 24; Mark 13; Luke 21.

- Wars and rumours of wars
- Nations rising against nations
- Earthquakes and famines
- Christians persecuted by synagogues
- The gospel is preached to all nations
- Men will hate Christians and betray them and have them put to death
- The abomination that causes desolation set up in Jerusalem
- False Christs and false prophets appear and deceive even the elect
- Christians in Judea are to flee to the mountains
- Cosmic signs in the heavens

Once again the meaning and timing of these signs is hotly debated, with different approaches contributing to the shape of the competing eschatological schemes. It is noticeable that the language used has a distinctly Jewish character, drawing on the eschatological and apocalyptic language of the Old Testament prophets. Some see these signs as already fulfilled, others as remaining to be fulfilled, whether in the present church age or in a period following the rapture of the church from the earth.

(iv) The Tribulation

Closely associated with the "last days" and the eschatological signs is the New Testament teaching which speaks of **a period of terrible suffering and persecution** that will precede the return of Christ. This "great tribulation" is found in the apocalyptic discourse of Jesus, and also in Revelation, where it is equated with a period of seven years in fulfilment of the prophecy of Daniel. Once again the timing and nature of this period of great suffering is highly contentious.

Matt 24:21

(v) The Antichrist

A number of New Testament texts also seem to suggest that the return of Jesus will be preceded by the appearance of a specific individual who will gather the world in rebellion to God and opposition to his people. 1 John 4:3 speaks of many antichrists who have already come, spreading false teaching that destroys the church, but that this will climax with the coming of "the" antichrist. In 2 Thessalonians, which is perhaps the most extensive consideration of eschatology in the Pauline corpus, Paul assures his readers that Jesus will not return until the "Man of Lawlessness" has been revealed, **who will be overthrown by the coming of Jesus**. Once again

2 Thess 2:1-10

the interpretation of these passages, whether they are referring to the same individual, and the timing of their fulfilment, is a matter of disagreement.

(vi) The Rapture

The rapture is the event described in 1 Thessalonians 4:17, in which Christian believers who are still alive and living on earth at the time that Jesus returns are taken to meet him in the air, and are transformed into the glorious state without the need to pass through death, so that they can join the other saints who are returning with him. The primary pastoral application of the rapture in this context is to reassure believers that Christians who have died before Jesus returns are safe with him and will share in the coming resurrection, and to prevent them from thinking that they will gain any advantage if they are still alive when he returns. The rapture has become a central and controlling feature of some eschatological schemes, especially dispensational pre-millennialism. Christians who take this view also find support in Jesus' apocalyptic discourse in Matt 24, where he speaks of how, prior to his return, "one will be taken and the other left." Without delving into the deeper interpretative issues, it is perhaps worth saying that this understanding of Matt 24 is highly questionable in its context, since Jesus is developing an analogy with the judgment at the time of the flood, and in that instance it is clear that being "taken" refers to being taken in judgment rather than being taken to be with Christ in order to escape judgment.

Matt 24:40-41

Matt 24:38-39

(vii) The future of Israel

A further very important element for any eschatological scheme concerns the future destiny of the Jews, and their relationship to the promised land. This question was raised by Jesus' disciples at the point of his ascension, and the nature of God's purposes for the Jews becomes very significant for Paul as his ministry increasingly concentrates on the Gentiles, who quickly outnumber Jewish converts in the church. Two key issues impact on eschatology.

First there is the question of whether the Old Testament promises made by God to Israel concerning their return to the physical land, and of the rebuilding of the Jerusalem temple, remain to be fulfilled. The Old Testament prophets certainly speak of an eschatological hope that is national, physical and geographic. Different eschatological schemes vary as to whether they think these promises remain to be fulfilled, or whether they are typological of a fuller and greater fulfilment in and through the church.

As for example in Ezek 37:15-48:35.

Second there is the distinct question of whether there will be a great conversion of many Jews to Christianity before Jesus returns. This depends upon the interpretation of Paul's teaching in Romans 9-11, and especially Romans 11:25-26 and his confidence that "all Israel will be saved." Some understand Paul to be saying that the present time is the "age of the Gentiles," during which time physical Israel will be largely hardened to the gospel and only a small remnant will be converted, but that when the Gentiles have "come in" either all the Jews at that time, or the vast majority of the Jews at that time, will be converted. Others regard Romans 9-11 as teaching the simultaneous ingathering of Jews and Gentiles into the church throughout the present "church age" as they respond to the gospel, so that the assertion that "all Israel will be saved" is a promise about the elect people of God as a whole. Gentile converts are grafted into Israel by faith, which makes them true children of

Gal 3:29 Abraham as well as sons of God.

(viii) The Millennium

Finally we come to the millennium, which is perhaps the most disputed of all the various components of eschatology, and has come to be regarded as the defining characteristic of the major eschatological schemes. The millennium is found in Revelation 20:1-6, and refers to a period of one thousand years, during which Christ will reign with his resurrected saints before the final coming of the new heavens and the new earth. There are multiple exegetical and interpretative issues regarding this passage, which crystallise the challenge of developing a coherent eschatology, and which highlight the deep differences that underlie the various competing schemes. These questions include:

For a detailed consideration of the exegetical issues see Darrell L. Bock, ed., *Three Views on the Millennium and Beyond* (Grand Rapids: Zondervan, 1999); G.K. Beale, *Revelation*, NIGTC (Grand Rapids: Eerdmans, 2013); Grant R. Osborne, *Revelation*, BECNT (Grand Rapids: Baker Academic, 2002).

➡ *Is the millennium a literal 1000 year period?*

➡ *Does the millennial reign of Christ and his saints take place on earth or in heaven?*

➡ *Have the saints who reign with Christ experienced bodily resurrection or spiritual resurrection?*

➡ *What does it mean that Satan has been bound so as not to deceive the nations?*

➡ *What does it mean that Satan will be released at the end of the millennium?*

➡ *When will the millennium take place – before or after the return of Christ?*

On top of these questions there is the challenge of determining what the millennium will be like. If Christ is to reign on earth with his saints for one thousand years ahead of the new creation, what will this period be like? Will people who have glorified resurrection bodies live alongside those who are still subject to death? How will people rebel against Jesus if he is physically present and glorified amongst them? Those who hold to a literal earthly reign of Christ and his saints find some support for the idea of the millennium from Old Testament prophecies that speak of an age of peace and justice that seems to be beyond anything experienced in the Old Testament or anticipated in the church age, but less than that which will be enjoyed in the new heavens and the new earth. Such passages speak, for example, of long life as a norm for humanity, but not of deliverance from physical death.

See for example Ps 72; Isa 11:6-11; 65:20; Zech 14:5-17.

Above all these issues, however, is the overriding question of whether the millennium is a distinct period of salvation history interposed between the present age and the eternal consummation of the kingdom in the new creation.

Underlying Presuppositions and Methodologies

This brief survey has revealed the extent of the challenge. The meaning of each of these elements is hotly contested, with dramatically different conclusions drawn. There is an inevitable circularity involved in some of the reasoning used to justify the various eschatological schemes, since the specific passages are often interpreted to fit with the overall scheme. The fact that there is such widespread disagreement on so many specifics ought to generate a degree of humility, and recognition that no eschatological scheme is obviously right in comparison to all the others. In evaluating and understanding the various schemes it is also essential to be aware of a number of broader questions of theology and biblical interpretation.

(i) Theological disciplines

The development of any eschatological scheme involves several different theological disciplines, all of which make an important contribution. An imbalance in the use of these tools will inevitably distort the scheme as a whole. We are engaged in an exercise of systematic theology, requiring the accurate exegesis of many individual texts, and the synthesis of the results into a coherent and logically consistent whole.

The contemporary over-emphasis on exegetical preaching and suspicion of systematic theology is yet another reason why eschatology is neglected in contemporary British evangelicalism.

However, systematic theology alone is not sufficient, as a biblically faithful eschatology will also require the tools of *biblical theology*, which describes the progressive nature of God's unfolding revelation of his plan of salvation, and teases out the continuities and discontinuities between the old covenant promises and their fulfilment in and through Christ.

(ii) Hermeneutics and Genre

Perhaps the most fundamental question that underlies the different eschatological schemes is whether biblical language is to be taken as literal, or whether it is in some sense figurative, symbolic or metaphorical. The underlying presupposition of some theologians is an overriding commitment to literalism in biblical interpretation, and deep suspicion of typology or symbolism. This determines, for example, whether the millennium is viewed as a literal period of one thousand years, or whether the number "one thousand" is symbolic of a long period of time. Another example concerns the language of cosmic signs that occurs in Jesus' apocalyptic discourse. Are we meant to think the stars will literally fall from the sky, or is this, in the light of Old Testament usage, symbolic language to describe the fall of great nations and overthrow of earthly political structures?

Isa 13:10; 34:4; Joel 2:10, 31.

Literalists sometimes start from the assumption that a spiritual or typological fulfilment of biblical prophesies is a liberalising downgrade of what was promised, whereas those who interpret such promises typologically regard the physical language a mere shadow of the greater and more glorious reality that has come through Christ.

(iii) Israel and the Church

The relationship between the nation of Israel and the Christian church is one of the most important issues underlying the different eschatological schemes. The different approaches might be categorised as: *distinction*; *replacement*; or *fulfilment*.

Those who argue for *distinction* maintain a strict separation between God's plans and promises for Israel and the church. To be true to himself, God must keep his covenant promises to Israel and the physical descendants of Abraham. On this approach the church is effectively a parenthesis in the plan of God for the salvation of the world that resulted from the Jews' rejection of Jesus as the Messiah. On his return the promises made to the Jewish nation will finally be fulfilled.

Those who argue for *replacement* assert that God's covenant promises have been transferred to the church because Israel rejected Jesus as Messiah. On this basis God no longer has any distinct promises to fulfil to Israel.

Finally, those who argue for *fulfilment* find a strong continuity between Israel and the church, and regard the promises to Israel as being fulfilled in the church as Jews and Gentiles alike put their faith in Jesus. It is not that Israel has been replaced by the church, but that Gentiles have been incorporated into Israel by faith so that they become the heirs of the promises, becoming true members of Abraham's family by faith. They would point to the many instances in which Old Testament language about physical Israel is used and applied to the church, and to the way in which both Israel and the church are the "assembly" of God's people, standing in direct continuity one from the other.

As, for example, in Acts 7:38 where Stephen describes Israel at Mount Sinai as "the church in the desert." For the continuity of Israel and the church see especially Eph 2:11-3:6.

(iv) Preterism or Futurism?

A final significant methodological difference concerns the timing of the fulfilment of the eschatological and apocalyptic texts in the New Testament. *Preterism* (from the Latin word *praeter* meaning 'past') regards these texts as having been fulfilled already in the events of the Jewish rebellion of A.D. 66-70, climaxing in the destruction of Jerusalem and the temple. The "signs" that precede and herald the "end of the age" have already occurred, and have ushered in the "church age" which is the final stage of salvation history. *Futurism* sees the texts as looking ahead to future events which have yet to occur and remain unfulfilled at present.

The matter is more complex because each of the main eschatological schemes can include aspects of a preterist understanding, leading to significant internal variation.

Major Eschatological Schemes

Having completed the essential groundwork of identifying the key events that need to be incorporated, and identifying the underlying methodological differences, we are now in a position to describe the major eschatological schemes that have emerged. These schemes are usually identified by the approach to the millennium, though they differ in regard to many other issues as well.

In fact they take their name from the way they relate the return of Jesus to the millennium. *Premillenialism* believes Jesus will return *before* the millennium; *postmillennialism* believes he will return *after* the millennium. As we'll see, *amillenialism* is a less helpful name for the view it describes.

(i) Classic Premillennialism

Classic premillennialism holds that the present church age will end with the rapture and physical return of Christ together with his resurrected and glorified saints to rule on earth for a period, which will end with the resurrection of the wicked, the final judgment and the new creation. The millennium is thus an intervening period between the church age and the eternal state during which Christ and his people rule on the earth. Classic premillennialism postulates a separation in time between the resurrection of the righteous and the resurrection of the wicked, which will occur at either end of the millennium.

e.g. Wayne Grudem, *Systematic Theology* (Leicester: IVP, 1994), 1111-1112, 1127-1131; Osborne, *Revelation*, 696-719.

Classic premillenialists differ as to whether they regard the millennium as a literal thousand year period, or whether this is symbolic of a lengthy time. Most classic premillennialists believe that the eschatological signs, including the great tribulation, remain to be fulfilled before Jesus can return, and that a great number of the Jews will be converted ahead of the millennium.

Classic premillennialism seems to have been the dominant view of the early church, but was largely eclipsed by the rise of amillennialism after Augustine, postmillennialism after the Reformation, and dispensational premillennialism in the mid-nineteenth century. Today it tends to be held largely by US evangelicals who have emerged from a dispensational and fundamentalist culture, but who have become Reformed in their views about salvation.

(ii) Dispensational Premillennialism

Dispensational premillennialism is not merely a variation of classic premillennialism, but an entirely different scheme that was developed in the mid-nineteenth century. It emerged as a result of the conviction that God must fulfil his promises to the Jews literally and physically, and maintains a sharp distinction between God's plans for Israel and the church. The overall scheme has been constructed to explain how such a fulfilment might be possible. Dispensational premillennialism became the dominant eschatological scheme amongst evangelicals between the late nineteenth and mid twentieth centuries, especially in America, and was closely associated with the rise of fundamentalism because it insists on a literal interpretation of Scripture.

Primarily by J.N. Darby, and then popularised by the Scofield Reference Bible.

Dispensational premillennialism teaches that at the end of the present church age Jesus will return secretly and rapture his people from the earth. There will then follow a period of seven years in which Israel will be re-established as a theocratic nation in literal fulfilment of the Old Testament prophecies, the temple rebuilt and sacrifices recommenced. This will also be the period of the great tribulation, during which the eschatological signs of the last days will be fulfilled. At the end of this period Jesus will return physically and visibly with his glorified people to establish his millennial kingdom on earth.

Within this broad overall scheme there are subtle variations as to when the rapture of the saints is expected to occur. The dominant view is that the rapture will occur before the great tribulation, which Christians will therefore be spared (*pre-trib*). Others, however, argue that the rapture will take place after the tribulation (*post-trib*), or that it will take place mid-way through the tribulation after a period of three and a half years (*mid-trib*).

Putting this together, this means that there are people who identify as: pre-trib premillenialists, post-trib premillenialists and mid-trib premillenialists. No wonder it gets confusing!

Dispensationalists know that they need to overcome the tension between passages that suggest that Jesus' return will be sudden and unexpected with those that suggest there will be preceding signs. They do so by separating the rapture from the bodily return of Christ, and locating the signs within the seven year period of the great tribulation. Dispensationalism thus stresses the urgency of evangelism, urging people to turn to Christ so that they will escape the pains of the great tribulation.

The implications of this radically different version of premillennialism are significant. For example, dispensational premillennialism inevitably means that vast swathes of the New Testament material, including the Sermon on the Mount and Jesus' apocalyptic discourse, are inapplicable to Christians because they concern the Jewish kingdom during the seven year period of the tribulation rather than the church. The same is true for much of the Old Testament, since the church is a parenthesis in distinction to Israel. Dispensationalism adopts the interpretative technique of "rightly dividing the word of truth," which seeks to differentiate between biblical passages that apply to Israel and those which apply to the church. Dispensationalists are also much more likely to regard events in the Middle East concerning the re-established state of Israel as signs that presage the rapture and the end-times events. Historically, dispensationalism has tended to dissuade Christians from the value of social action and seeking to improve the state of society, or from environmental concern and creation care, as these are unnecessary if the time of eschatological fulfilment is thought to be imminent.

(iii) Amillennialism

Amillennialism is something of a misnomer, as the name might suggest that it rejects the idea of a millennium at all. Rather, amillennialism equates the millennium of Rev 20:1-6 with the current church age, so that we can say that we are currently living in the millennium, which is the final era of salvation history. Jesus will return at the end of this period, when the rapture will occur and the dead will be raised and judged. Strictly speaking, amillenialism is therefore postmillennial, in that the return of Jesus will follow after the millennium has occurred.

For a highly detailed consideration of amillenialism see Beale, *Revelation*, 972-1021.

Within this broad scheme there is vast variation. Some amillennialists are also preterists, regarding the eschatological signs as having been fulfilled in the first century; others regard the "last days" as the entire period of the church age; still others see the "last days" as the final period of the church age, equating to the final Satanic rebellion described in Revelation 20:6 at the end of the millennium. Amillennialists also vary as to their convictions about the future of Israel and the Jews, with some anticipating a mass conversion of Jewish people at the end of the millennium and others expecting the conversion of a remnant of Jewish people throughout the church age. Amillennialists see the millennium as a period of both gospel growth but also opposition and persecution for Christians. They differ, however, on the degree to which they believe that the gospel will triumph and the scale of gospel response and societal transformation we can expect.

Amillennialism was the dominant eschatology of the church from the time of Augustine to the Puritan period in the sixteenth century, and has recovered to become the predominant position of contemporary British evangelicals standing in the Reformed tradition.

(iv) Postmillennialism

See Iain H. Murray, *Revival and the Interpretation of Prophecy* (Edinburgh: Banner of Truth 1971); Keith A. Mathison, *Postmillennialism: An Eschatology of Hope* (Phillipsburg: Presbyterian and Reformed, 1999); Bebbington, *The Dominance of Evangelicalism*, 130-132.

Postmillennialism is a significantly more triumphalist variant of amillennialism. In common with amillennialism, it holds that Jesus will return after the millennium has occurred, but unlike amillenialism it does not equate the millennium with the present church age. Post-millennialism anticipates overwhelming gospel success during the church age, which will see the conversion of a great proportion of humanity, ushering in an era of overwhelming Christian influence leading to a period of peace and prosperity. The millennium will not, on this understanding, involve the physical rule of Christ on earth, but his spiritual rule on earth through the church to an unprecedented degree. At the end of the millennium there will be a satanic rebellion against God and his rule, which will be quelled by the rapture and return of Jesus with his glorified and resurrected saints.

Postmillennialism is also subject to significant internal variation, with divergent views on the timing of the "last days" and the future for the Jews. Perhaps a preterist view that sees the eschatological signs fulfilled in the first century sits most comfortably with the overall approach of postmillennialism, as this would mean that the biblical texts that speak of great suffering for the people of God have already been fulfilled, thus allowing for the emergence of a glorious period of gospel advance and the peace and prosperity of the church.

Postmillennialism emerged as the dominant eschatological position of Christians during the Puritan period, and then again after the evangelical revivals of the eighteenth and nineteenth century. It coincided with significant gospel progress and improvements in society and culture associated with the Enlightenment and scientific advance. It provided much of the impetus for the modern missionary movement and the social and political engagement of evangelicals seeking to reform society. The liberal social gospel of humanistic advance was its secular offspring. It began to wane in the second half of the nineteenth century when the church began to decline through the impact of liberalism, and was largely supplanted by dispensational premillennialism as the world descended into horrific war in the early years of the twentieth century. Apostasy and false teaching in the church, coupled with escalating wickedness and conflict in the world, made postmillennialism seem implausible but it has seen a revival in more recent decades, especially amongst Presbyterians.

Conclusion

It has been seen that there are a number or eschatological schemes, or perhaps more accurately families of eschatological schemes, that are held by evangelical Christians.

Even though eschatology is a relatively neglected concern in contemporary British evangelicalism, it inevitably exerts a considerable influence on our evangelical culture, and helps to explain differences in approach to the mission of the church. For that reason, some evaluation and reflection are called for.

(i) Evaluation

All of the eschatological positions have their strengths, and have been developed with honest motives and good intentions. They all have some weak points, where they struggle to accommodate some of the biblical data.

- I find dispensational premillennialism unconvincing because it misconstrues the relationship between Israel and the church and fails to appreciate typological fulfilment of the old covenant in the new.

- I find the postmillennial position unconvincing in its handling of Rev 20:1-6, viewing the millennium as the earthly influence of the church. It seems doubtful that any first century reader would have understood the text in this way. Postmillennialism seems to me to read experiences of gospel growth at specific moments of history into the text, rather than to interpret the text on its own terms.

- I find considerable strength and plausibility in both classical premillennialism and amillennialism, which are very similar in their understanding of the current church age.

- I find the premillennial interpretation of Old Testament prophecies as describing the millennial kingdom, rather than as typological foreshadowing of the new creation, unconvincing.

- I regard premillennialism as less plausible because of the lack of any other clear biblical support outside of Revelation 20:1-6 for a separation between the physical resurrections of the righteous and the wicked, or for an earthly reign of Christ between the church age and the new creation. One would have expected much wider biblical attestation for something of such significance to the unfolding of salvation history, especially given the high volume of eschatological teaching in the gospels and epistles.

- Whilst I am largely persuaded by the amillennial position, which can incorporate many of the best insights of both classical premillennialism and postmillennialism, I fear that it may not do adequate justice to Revelation 20:1-6, since it supposes that the early Christians would have anticipated that the church age would endure for a very considerable period, and this seems less easy to reconcile with their prayer "Come Lord Jesus." Rev 22:20

(ii) Wider Reflections

Eschatology and Gospel Unity

Although eschatology has sometimes proved divisive between evangelicals, it is remarkable that evangelical unity can be maintained despite widely divergent eschatological understanding. Most evangelicals treat the exact unfolding of salvation history as a secondary matter that should not subvert their unity in those things of "first importance." This unity is made possible because evangelicals are essentially agreed that we are currently living in the church age, and that our task is to preach the gospel to all nations in anticipation of the next stage of salvation history, whatever that may be.

Divisions between evangelicals over issues of eschatology are very often a result of more fundamental disagreement over methodologies and matters of biblical interpretation. Dispensational premillennialists may therefore dismiss amillennialists or postmillennialists because they believe that they have abandoned a commitment to biblical inerrancy by adopting "spiritual" rather than "literal" interpretations. Amillennialists may dismiss premillennialists because they regard them as guilty of a crass literalism or of a faulty understanding of the relationship between Israel and the church, which then undermines the finished work of Christ by suggesting that there is a need for the sacrificial system to be resumed at some future point.

In practice, gospel unity will be easiest between those whose positions, and mission priorities, are most similar. Amillenialists and classic premillennialists often have far more in common with each other than either has with dispensational premillennialists or postmillennialists.

Eschatology and Evangelical Psychology

See Richard Lovelace, *The Dynamics of Spiritual Renewal* (Leicester: IVP, 1979), 401-416.

There is a symbiotic relationship between eschatology and the psychology of evangelicals, and whether they are optimistic or pessimistic about the prospects for the church in the world. It is less clear whether psychology determines eschatology, or whether eschatology influences the psychology of wider evangelical culture. It is certainly the case that postmillennialism has come to the fore when the gospel has been clearly advancing and seeming to triumph within society. In contrast, when the church is under attack or declining, dispensational premillennialism has gained the upper hand. Amillennialism and classical premillennialism are less susceptible to the vagaries of church growth or decline, since they expect both gospel growth and ongoing persecution and resistance to the rule of Christ in the church age.

Eschatology and the Church's Mission

Although evangelicals of all eschatological persuasions are committed to the task of evangelism in the present age, the eschatalogical scheme they adopt inevitably influences their approach to the mission of the church and the way that they undertake it. Postmillennialists are more likely to be committed not just to evangelism but to the transformation of culture and society through the influence of the church, as they believe that this will usher in the millennial age. For this reason theonomists, who see the Christian mission as the implementation of biblical law in society, tend to be postmillennial in their eschatology. Furthermore, postmillenialists may have a strong expectation of revival as the means by which God will accomplish his purpose. They are likely to take a longer term view of the church's work, investing in institutions and infrastructure that will advance the cause of the gospel over the generations.

In contrast, dispensational premillennialists live with the conviction that the rapture could occur at any moment, which drives an urgency in evangelism to encourage people to escape the coming tribulation. However, especially if there is a heightened expectation that we are living in the last days, this can lead to a withdrawal from the concerns of political and cultural life, and make investment in long term projects seem futile. Futurists, whether dispensational premillennialists, classic premillennialists or amillennialists, can all become unduly focused on seeking to "read the signs" that will herald the coming of the "last days" and presage whatever event they believe will follow them. Much effort has been spent on futile speculation, with consequent disappointment and disillusionment.

Eschatology and Pastoral Ministry

Eschatology cannot be avoided in pastoral ministry and church leadership, and it compels pastors and teachers to come to settled convictions. Virtually every book of the Bible includes eschatological elements, and many of the New Testament letters set their exhortations in an eschatological framework. It is impossible to preach expository sermons without engaging with eschatology, and a pure agnosticism is neither possible nor helpful to God's people.

However, above and beyond the specific details of eschatology, we need never to lose sight of the primary pastoral purpose of the eschatological teaching of Jesus and the apostles. Eschatological and apocalyptic material is not there to provide Christians with a road-map of geopolitical events, as if it were a complex code to crack, but rather to provide hope in the face of adversity, and to encourage faithful service of Jesus in the present moment. It is intended to give confidence that Jesus will triumph over evil and wickedness, and that he will return to establish his kingdom on earth. In the meantime we are to work hard as his servants, loving and caring for one another and labouring to grow his kingdom by preaching the gospel. Any eschatological scheme that leads to introspective speculation, fear of what the future might hold for God's people, or passivity because it is not thought to be worthwhile to work because the Lord's return is imminent, clearly fails to reflect the New Testament teaching. ₽

e.g. 2 Thess 1:5-10.
e.g. 1 Cor 15:58.

GREATER GRACE

An excerpt from Augustine's *City of God* with an introduction and annotations by Bradley G. Green.

Augustine is perhaps the most important figure in the history of Christian thought. Other contenders might be Athanasius, Thomas Aquinas, Calvin, and Luther, but any list of the great thinkers of the Christian tradition must include Augustine, who lived from A.D. 354-430. He bequeathed to the Church a dizzying literary output, with *City of God* perhaps being the jewel of his writings.

In the early years of the fifth century, Rome and its influence had grown. But so had the Christian faith. In A.D. 410 the Visigoth Alaric had successfully invaded Rome, but after a few days Alaric and his men left the city. Rome had not been fully conquered (i.e. destroyed), but nonetheless, it had been shown to be vulnerable. At least some people thought the Christian faith was to blame for Rome's weakness, for its susceptibility to invasion. Apparently these types of criticisms

A woodcut of Augustine from a 1489 edition of *City of God*.

ETERNAL LEISURE

were circulating, and led Augustine to take up his pen. The result – written from A.D. 413-427 – was the *City of God*.

Whether one wants to call *City of God* a philosophy or theology of history, or a philosophy or history of the church, or even a kind of biblical theology of sorts, it is a monumental achievement, and is more than any of those descriptors. For Augustine covers virtually every important doctrine of Christian theology in this work. And this includes eschatology – which for Augustine is virtually the substructure of Christian theology. For Augustine, history is going somewhere, and has been doing so since the first moment of creation. Augustine's "tale of two cities" plots out the origin, growth, and end of the two cities. These two cities – the city of God and the city of man – are shorthand for believers (the city of God) and for those who will persist in unbelief (the city of man), although it should be noted that the city of God and the city of man can also signify (1) humanity's ultimate destiny (the city of God), and (2) the day-to-day realities of earthly existence (the city of man). These two cities exist side-by-side in a sense, and are intermingled in the present. The city of God will one day flower into its fullness, while the city of man awaits judgment and destruction.

In the selection that follows we see a number of Augustine's insights and convictions come together: the nature of true freedom, the ultimately end or *telos* of redeemed persons, and some of Augustine's thoughts on what the new creation will be like. The selection is the last few pages of the last book of Augustine's *City of God*. Up to this point, Augustine has outlined the origin, growth, and end of the two cities. Here he is bringing his massive work to an end, and speaking of the new creation, or the future state of Christians.

CITY OF GOD

BOOK 22, CHAPTER 30

Notice here that in the future state of Christians we are neither "halted by idleness" nor "driven by need." Augustine seems to be saying that in our future state it is impossible to be idle, for we will be so consumed with praising the Triune God that idleness is a conceptual impossibility. Neither will there be "need," because need implies some lack which must be dealt with. But in our future state we will truly be the persons we were designed to be – those who praise and love God – and thus there is no "need" in the life of the believer.

We simply note here that Augustine sees the future state in terms of "felicity" (we might today speak of a true and deep "happiness"). This is contrasted with "necessity" – and like we said of "need" above, there are no such needs (or necessities) in the future state of the believer.

How great shall be that happiness, which shall be tainted with no evil, which shall lack no good, and which shall afford leisure for the praises of God, who shall be all in all! For I know not what other employment there can be where no weariness shall slacken activity, nor any need stimulate to labour. I am admonished also by the sacred song, in which I read or hear the words, "Blessed are those who dwell in your house; they are ever praising you." (Ps 84:4)

Wholesome bodies in whole-hearted worship

All the members and organs of the incorruptible body, which now we see to be suited to various necessary uses, shall contribute to the praises of God; for in that life necessity shall have no place, but full, certain, secure, everlasting felicity. For all those parts of the bodily harmony, which are distributed through the whole body, within and without, and of which I have just been saying that they at present elude our observation, shall then be discerned; and, along with the other great and marvellous discoveries which shall then kindle rational minds in praise of the great

It is important to note how Augustine speaks of "rational." Our age often either (1) denigrates the importance of rationality (seen in different forms of feeling-based religion, or ethical emotivism, or anti-intellectualism – inside and outside the church) or (2) elevates too uncritically the use of reason (in various forms of philosophical naturalism, atheism, etc.). Augustine – as the best of the Christian tradition – really does neither. Notice how "rational minds" are "set on fire." There is a proper kind of passion in using reason rightly. True reason is not cold, "calculating," or set apart from the affections. Protestants wanting to affirm properly both the affections and reason can learn a lot from Augustine.

Creator, there shall be the enjoyment of a beauty which appeals to the reason. What power of movement such bodies shall possess, I have not the audacity rashly to define, as I have not the ability to conceive. Nevertheless I will say that in any case, both in motion and at rest, they shall be, as in their appearance, seemly; for into that state nothing which is unseemly shall be admitted.

Notice that Augustine is a tad wary of saying too much about our future state. There is a proper kind of caution which should be used as one speaks about the future state of Christians.

Above we saw Augustine speak of the "proportion," here of things being "fitting." In the future state all will be as it ought to be, and for Augustine this can be spoken of in terms of proportion and fittingness.

God as our greatest desire and reward

One thing is certain, the body shall forthwith be wherever the spirit wills, and the spirit shall will nothing which is unbecoming either to the spirit or to the body. True honour shall be there, for it shall be denied to none who is worthy, nor yielded to any unworthy; neither shall any unworthy person so much as sue for it, for none but the worthy shall be there. True peace shall be there, where no one shall suffer opposition either from himself or any other. God himself, who is the Author of virtue, shall there be its reward; for, as there is nothing greater or better, he has promised himself. What else was meant by his word through the prophet, "I will be your God and you will be my people," (Jer 7:23) than, I shall be their satisfaction, I shall be all that men honourably desire: life, and health, and nourishment, and plenty, and glory, and honour, and

The ultimate reward which Christians look forward to receiving is God himself. There is of course nothing greater which can be received. And of course God gives himself as a gift. God is the only ultimate end of our desires, the object of our most crucial "seeing," "loving," and "praising."

peace, and all good things? This, too, is the right interpretation of the saying of the apostle, "so that God may be all in all" (1 Cor 15:28). He shall be the end of our desires who shall be seen without end, loved without tiring, praised without weariness. This outgoing of affection, this employment, shall certainly be, like eternal life itself, common to all.

Universal contentment with different rewards

But who can conceive, not to say describe, what degrees of honour and glory shall be awarded to the various degrees of merit? Yet it cannot be doubted that there shall be degrees. And in that blessed city there shall be this great blessing, that no inferior shall envy any superior, as now the archangels are not envied by the angels, because no one will wish to be what he has not received, though bound in strictest concord with him who has received; as in the body the finger does not seek to be the eye, though both members are harmoniously included in the complete structure of the body. And thus, along with his gift, greater or less, each shall receive this further gift of contentment to desire no more than he has.

The freedom of a will unable to sin

Neither are we to suppose that because sin shall have no power to delight them, free will must be withdrawn. It will, on the contrary, be all the more truly free, because set free from delight in sinning to take unfailing delight in not sinning. For the first freedom of will, which

What Augustine says here about "the merits deserving of reward" can be vexing to many Christians – especially Protestants. Many Christians – Catholics and Protestants in their different ways – have tended to speak of the Christian's relationship to God in terms of "merit": Protestants by emphasising that Christ "merited" our salvation on our behalf, and Rome by emphasising that God helps us to merit our own salvation. But "reward" itself appears too often in Scripture to simply be dismissed. If one reads the writings of Augustine, a central truth emerges which is helpful. While God does reward his people, his reward is always "crowning his own gifts." That is, God does reward us, but he is crowning in us the gifts he has given us freely, which he gave us apart from any sort of merit or earning of the gifts. God indeed "rewards" his people by crowning (rewarding) us. But he is crowning (rewarding) something he gave us freely apart from works!

In the future state one is enjoying the gifts of God all the way down. There is even the gift of being content with the gifts one has been given, even if one has not been given the gifts of the next person!

One of Augustine's most precious insights into the future state: We will not be able to sin, but not because we are not free, but because we are most fully free.

man received when he was created upright, consisted in an ability not to sin, but also in an ability to sin; whereas this last freedom of will shall be superior, inasmuch as it shall not be able to sin. This, indeed, shall not be a natural ability, but the gift of God. For it is one thing to be God, another thing to be a partaker of God. God by nature cannot sin, but the partaker of God receives this inability from God. And in this divine gift there was to be observed this gradation, that man should first receive a free will by which he was able not to sin, and at last a free will by which he was not able to sin – the former being adapted to the acquiring of merit, the latter to the enjoying of the reward. But the nature thus constituted, having sinned when it had the ability to do so, it is by a more abundant grace that it is delivered so as to reach that freedom in which it cannot sin. For as the first immortality which Adam lost by sinning consisted in his being able not to die, while the last shall consist in his not being able to die; so the first free will consisted in his being able not to sin, the last in his not being able to sin. And thus piety and justice shall be as unassailable as happiness. For certainly by sinning we lost both piety and happiness; but when we lost happiness, we did not lose the love of it. Are we to say that God himself is not free because he cannot sin?

In that city, then, there shall be free will, one in all the citizens, and indivisible in each, delivered from all ill, filled with all good, enjoying the unassailable delights of eternal joys, oblivious of sins, oblivious of sufferings, and yet not so oblivious of its deliverance as to be ungrateful to its Deliverer.

i.e. Adam

...BY SINNING WE LOST BOTH PIETY AND HAPPINESS; BUT WHEN WE LOST HAPPINESS, WE DID NOT LOSE THE LOVE OF IT.

In the new creation there is **true** freedom and **true** delight. Note what Augustine is trying to hold together: We are so free from our sins and failings that we are "oblivious of sufferings." Nonetheless, we can be thankful for our deliverance from our sins and failings.

WE SHALL HAVE ETERNAL LEISURE TO SEE THAT HE IS GOD...

Again, in the new creation the believer is so thoroughly freed from sin and the experience of being trapped in sin, that the believer has "forgotten" the past. In this first sense the believer's former ways have been "blotted out of their experience." But in another sense, what Augustine calls "intellectual knowledge", the believer remembers their past woes, and that they have been rescued.

The memory of past sin and our knowledge of hell

The soul, then, shall have an intellectual remembrance of its past ills; but, so far as regards sensible experience, they shall be quite forgotten. For a skilful physician knows, indeed, professionally almost all diseases; but experimentally he is ignorant of a great number which he himself has never suffered from.

As, therefore, there are two ways of knowing evil things – one by mental insight, the other by sensible experience, for it is one thing to understand all vices by the wisdom of a cultivated mind, another to understand them by the foolishness of an abandoned life – so also there are two ways of forgetting evils. For a well-instructed and learned man forgets them one way, and he who has experimentally suffered from them forgets them another, the former by neglecting what he has learned, the latter by escaping what he has suffered. And in this latter way the saints shall forget their past ills, for they shall have so thoroughly escaped them all, that they shall be quite blotted out of their experience. But their intellectual knowledge, which shall be great, shall keep them acquainted not only with their own past woes, but with the eternal sufferings of the lost. For if they were not to know that they had been miserable, how could they, as the Psalmist says, for ever sing the mercies of God? Certainly that city shall have no greater joy than the celebration of the grace of Christ, who redeemed us by his blood.

Our Sabbath rest

There shall be accomplished the words of the psalm, "Be still, and know that I am God" (Ps 46:10). There shall be the great Sabbath, which has no evening, which God celebrated among his first works, as it is written, "on the seventh day he rested from all his work. Then God blessed the seventh day and made it holy, because on it he rested from all the work of creating that he had done," (Gen 2:2-3). For we shall ourselves be the seventh day, when we shall be filled and replenished with God's blessing and sanctification. There shall we be still, and know that he is God; that he is that which we ourselves aspired to be when we fell away from him, and listened to the voice of the seducer, "You will be like God" (Gen 3:5) and so abandoned God, who would have made us as gods, not by deserting him, but by participating in him. For without him what have we accomplished, save to perish in his anger? But when we are restored by him, and perfected with greater grace, we shall have eternal leisure to see that he is God, for we shall be full of him when he shall be all in all.

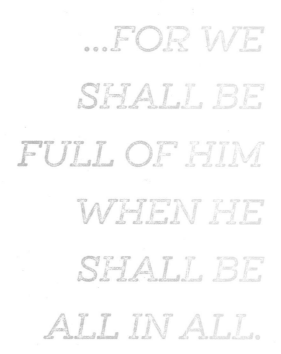

...FOR WE SHALL BE FULL OF HIM WHEN HE SHALL BE ALL IN ALL.

For Augustine, the ultimate end or telos of the believer is to see God, and rest in seeing him.

For further reading...

If you want to read more of Augustine, *City of God* repays reading. Our selection is from the last book (we might say "chapter"), 22, and is worth the reader's time. If you want to start with a shorter work of Augustine, you might start with *Enchiridion*, which sometimes has the English word "manual" in the title. It is a kind of "mini" systematic theology. If you want to explore Augustine on grace, Nick Needham's *The Triumph of Grace: Augustine's Writings on Salvation* (London: Evangelical Press, 2000) is a gold-mine. Although it might not at first sound too inviting, sitting down with a cup of coffee and perusing *Augustine Through the Ages: An Encyclopaedia* (Grand Rapids: Eerdmanns, 2009), is a lot of fun. It has excellent, short entries on all the key aspects of Augustine's thought, with first-rate bibliographies. The standard, and still excellent, biography is Peter Brown's *Augustine of Hippo* (London: Faber and Faber, 1975, though it's worth getting the updated 2000 edition that includes discussion of the sermons and letters of Augustine discovered since 1975). P

QUENCHING THE FLAMES?

Adrian Reynolds engages with some recent books on hell.

John Piper's 2011 tweet was a withering dismissal of Rob Bell's controversial book *Love Wins: heaven, hell and the fate of every person who ever lived*. Bell's book – "full of confusing half truths" – seemed to suggest that universalism (the belief that everybody will be saved) was an orthodox evangelical belief which should be more widely embraced. The Christian world responded rapidly and strongly at both a popular and scholarly level. Most assumed that Piper's putdown was part of this direct response to the downgrade of the doctrine of hell that Bell espoused.

Derek Tidball, review of *Love Wins*, Evangelical Alliance website, *www.eauk.org*, 29 March 2011.

It wasn't until much later that Piper clarified his tweet. Interviewed by Justin Taylor on *The Gospel Coalition* blog in March 2012, Piper explained that his objection was not so much Bell's view of hell in and of itself but that he found Bell's "cynicism about the cross of the Lord Jesus Christ" placed him outside of orthodox belief. Indeed, argued Piper, he would disagree with John Stott on the doctrine of hell, yet "I would have sat at his feet until the day he died."

Available on *thegospelcoalition.org*, 30 March 2012. Search 'farewell rob bell'.

Inside and outside the camp

Bell's book, the response from the Christian world and – especially – Piper's tweet encapsulates some of the difficulties when it comes to the doctrine of hell. Broadly speaking, there are views of hell that are outside normal Christian belief (and which, arguably, disqualify you from owning the label *evangelical*) and there are others which, whilst held strongly, are within the camp.

Perhaps Stott typifies this tension best of all. When John Stott revealed that he had some sympathy with the position known as Conditional Immortality (of which more in a moment), one honest writer exclaimed, "I thought John Stott was a Christian!" And yet, as Piper implies, such views do not disqualify him as an evangelical, but are considered within the bounds of what we commonly identify as orthodox belief.

Preston Sprinkle, *Four Views on Hell* (Grand Rapids, Michigan: Zondervan, 2016), 9.

The debate (which is significantly older than the Rob Bell debacle) has led to a large number of books and this short article seeks to bring the discussion to readers through brief interaction with some of the key volumes that are produced at a popular or basic scholarly level. I will seek to explain some of the views and explore some of the key issues the debate raises, alongside some practical applications (which are often neglected in the material).

What do people believe?

Ed. Preston Sprinkle, *Four Views on Hell: Second Edition* (Grand Rapids, Michigan: Zondervan, 2016).

Open theism is a movement which diminishes the sovereignty of God, particularly over future events. God is not sovereign and though he is better at guessing the future than you or I, he has no control over it.

I will start with the most helpful book for defining our terms. *Four Views on Hell*, edited by Preston Sprinkle, is a 2016 edition of an older 1996 volume. Apart from the title, the two share almost nothing in common. In his introduction, Sprinkle argues that a new volume is required due to the fact that previously outside-the-camp positions are now considered mainstream. However, more has changed in the 20 years between editions. The 1996 volume was philosophical in its approach, giving as much time to logic and reason as to making a biblical case. It is less readable (and persuasive) as a result. Moreover, one of the contributors, the late Clark Pinnock, has since become associated with the open theism movement and his name is probably a burden to the volume. It needed to be replaced.

The new edition takes a more straightforward approach, listing four views on hell and then – as with all of the volumes in this series – letting the authors make their case biblically before engaging with each other to a certain degree. It is not surprising that the benefit of reading such a book is not necessarily the essays themselves but the ways that the authors pick up on each other's arguments and critique them. The four positions are:

Eternal conscious torment (ECT): Hell is a physical place where the wicked and rebellious will experience everlasting conscious punishment. This is what we might also call the historical view (though some opponents unsurprisingly reject this assessment of history). This view is consistent with the everlasting language found in Scripture.

Conditional immortality (CI) also called conditionalism, conditional annihilationism or terminal punishment: Hell is still a physical place of punishment, but it is not everlasting and, at some moment, this punishment will come to an end and the individual will cease to be. This view does more justice to the destruction language used of hell in the Bible.

Evangelical universalism combines elements of both of these positions, but argues (especially on the basis of Eph. 1:10) that, at some point in the future, everything will be reconciled under Christ, and so – ultimately – even those punished will be saved to the new creation and new earth.

In a fourth, rather odd, chapter, one author argues for the reinstatement of **a revised doctrine of purgatory** as being acceptable within evangelical orthodoxy.

The careful reader cannot help thinking that the last two positions have essentially been included to 'balance the books' and ensure that there are still four views to present. This reviewer, at least, cannot see how these last two positions are orthodox in any meaningful sense of the word, and therefore including them in this volume serves little purpose other than to muddy the waters.

Indeed, another book in a similar series from IVP Academic ignores them all together. *Two Views of Hell* by Edward Fudge (CI) and Robert Peterson (ECT) is therefore more substantial because it lets the two main positions interact with each other without the confusion of extreme minority positions. The volume predates the Rob Bell debate (it was published in 2000) but is no less useful for that. There is also a helpful sharpness in the responses in this second volume that is sometimes lacking in the first. It is a better book than *Four Views* in almost every way.

Edward William Fudge & Robert A. Peterson, *Two Views of Hell* (Downers Grove, Illinois: InterVarsity Press, 2000).

It is worth noting that neither of the two main positions denies the existence of hell as a physical place, nor the reality of hell as a place of unmentionable awfulness. The caricature of CI is that it downplays hell and, therefore, evangelism, offering people a sneaky way out of the consequences of their sin. Whilst there may be proponents of this position for whom that is true, none of the contributors of these volumes take this stance. Hell is real and terrible and each of the authors quakes at its reality.

This debate within the evangelical camp, therefore, is not about the *existence* of hell itself, nor even of the *nature* of hell. The question, rather, is on the *extent* of hell or, to put it in biblical terms, what does Jesus save us from when he promises that "everyone who believes in Him *will not* perish" (John 3:16).

Two views in the church

How common are these views (particularly CI) in the church today? The orthodox position is well-represented in most historical statements of faith. The Westminster Confession of Faith (Chapter XXXIII) and 1689 London Baptist Confession (chapter 32) are both clear. Some opponents of the doctrine claim that the everlasting nature of hell is not required as a doctrine in the Anglican church for, whilst it was in the original 42 Articles, it does not appear in the 39. However, the homilies and liturgy accompanying the Articles make clear that ECT was always in view. The briefer FIEC doctrinal basis includes the statement that "the wicked will be sent to eternal punishment."

I am grateful to Lee Gatiss of Church Society for this insight. For example, the Book of Common Prayer burial service includes the line "deliver us not into the bitter pains of eternal death."

ACUTE, *The Nature of Hell* (London: Paternoster, 2000). Now out of print, but second hand copies are easy to source.

A report by the Evangelical Alliance Commission on Unity and Truth Among Evangelicals (ACUTE) published in 2000 under the title *The Nature of Hell* is very helpful in charting the historic background, including an honest assessment of how the EA statement of faith itself has been amended, almost certainly to incorporate both views. Now out of print, this useful book is extraordinarily clear in outlining the various positions, their strengths and weaknesses, and biblical foundations. Whilst not including the interaction of *Four Views* and *Two Views*, a reader would gain a comprehensive insight into the debate.

The EA has also surveyed their churches to discover how firmly the two main views are held. The data is now reasonably out of date (the survey was conducted in 1998). Of those churches who responded, 80% affirmed ECT, whilst 14% affirmed CI. This latter figure may have subsequently declined with the growth of majority churches in the UK where historic soteriology and views of hell are often the norm.

Despite some protestations, it is clear that ECT is the historic position as the ACUTE report (and almost every other book reviewed) makes clear. Although it is possible to find some historical figures who questioned ECT, it is hard work and quotes and references are few and far between. As one opponent honestly admits, "It is clear where the overwhelming consensus lies in the history of theology and that is why... the burden of proof remains on those who reject the traditional doctrine of hell as conscious eternal misery."

Four Views, 55.

Making the case?

Each of the books I surveyed does a respectable job of setting out the biblical case for ECT. In *Four Views* Denny Burk (who serves on the faculty of Boyce College at Southern Seminary in the US) does a workmanlike job of taking readers through ten key texts to make his case. He begins his argument, however, with a story to illustrate a point that is often made in defence of ECT. "The seriousness of sin – and thus the punishment due to sin – is not measured merely by the sin itself but by the value and the worth of the one sinned against."

Four Views, 19.

In critiquing his argument, CI proponent John Stackhouse not only takes issue with the interpretation of individual texts (as one might imagine), but challenges this foundational statement in strong language. "The actual data of Scripture are entirely against him." This is clearly overstated, but it is true that the argument based on God's infinite worth is never made explicit in Scripture. However, the same is also true of many of the arguments against ECT, for example that it would be unjust for God to judge finite sins with

Four Views, 45.

infinite punishment; moreover, the death of Christ was a finite act that came to an end, so the punishment for which Calvary is a substitute should also have a terminus in view.

In fact, Stackhouse's case for CI is less convincing than that of his fellow advocate Fudge in the *Two Views* volume, probably because Stackhouse has less space and is operating at a more populist level. His argument is undermined by the use of pejorative language such as describing God as "torturing" rather than the more biblical "punishing" or "judging." Moreover, he surely overstates his case: "I make bold to contend, nonetheless, that terminal punishment [CI] enjoys about as strong a warrant in Scripture as I have seen can be offered for any doctrine." Such a claim is clearly unwarranted when one considers a host of other core beliefs.

Fudge offers a much more considered argument in *Two Views*. He makes his case through a survey of the Old Testament, the words of Jesus, the writings of Paul and then a catch-all "rest of the New Testament." To his credit, he is crystal clear on the reality of hell, quoting Jonathan Edwards, Charles Spurgeon and Billy Graham – lamenting along the way that preachers say so little on a subject about which Scripture says so much. Yet he maintains that the Bible teaches a conditional view. This is unsurprising, he argues, as the notion of an immortal soul is not a biblical one, but one borrowed from Greek philosophy.

A matter of perspective

It is unavoidable that some of the biblical language best supports ECT (especially the vocabulary of *everlasting*) whilst other biblical data supports CI (especially the language of *destruction*) and so a curious but intriguing middle ground has been proposed in an article in *The Churchman* published in 1996. Douglas Spanner, an ordained vicar and an Emeritus Professor at the University of London, argued that Einstein's theory of relativity may be helpful! Scientists understand that matter entering a black hole ceases to exist or continues to exist depending on your point of view. From the point of view of an observer, the black hole swallows matter completely – it is *destroyed*. But from the point of view of the matter itself, there is no end to existence, it is *everlasting*. Sci-fi fans everywhere can rejoice at the illustration as they imagine a spaceship entering the void! Spanner argues that this insight may throw some light onto the apparently conflicting language in the Scriptures to describe the same thing – the vocabulary of destruction and eternality is equally true and relevant, *it just depends on your observation point*. In other words, to an outside observer (if such a thing existed), hell is destructive. However to the one experiencing its justice, it is everlasting.

"Is Hell Forever?" *Churchman* 110.2 (1996), 107-20, available as a PDF online.

What issues are at stake?

Herein lie some of the challenges for us thinking these issues through. Ultimately this debate is not about what we believe about the extent of hell, but our views on a whole host of other key doctrines. Remember Piper's tweet? Rob Bell will be forever remembered as the man who questioned the existence of hell. Yet Piper's objection was that he was too cavalier with the doctrine of the cross. In Stackhouse's CI argument we see again that, when it comes to doctrine, everything is connected to everything. Doctrines are not believed or disbelieved in isolation from one another. They shape and inform one another. Critical to them all is our doctrine of God himself, our humanity (both created and fallen) and the Cross of Christ which redeems us.

Perhaps most importantly, it is almost impossible to grapple with the extent of hell without interacting with another key doctrine – the immortality of the soul (a question which looms large in the debate) and the nature of sin itself (on this, see *Primer* issue 02).

It is for this reason, rather than the biblical data alone, that I am ultimately unconvinced by the CI argument. I accept that other proponents of CI have not softened their stance on key connected doctrines, but the logical implications of adopting this position seem, to me at least, to threaten what we believe on other critical matters.

Francis Chan & Preston Sprinkle, *Erasing Hell* (Colorado Springs, Colorado: David C. Cook, 2011).

Some of the other responses to Bell, written with varying depth and with differing readerships in mind, make these connections clearly and helpfully. I found Francis Chan and Preston Sprinkle's *Erasing Hell* one of the best. The first time I read this through I found it frustrating in style and somewhat patronising. However, on a second reading, I've either become simpler myself or (I hope) wiser in understanding what is needed in a book that can counter a popular argument.

This, then, is not an academic tome. But it is surprisingly comprehensive, answering relatively deep questions – for example about the nature of justice in the Bible. The authors are generally gracious in pointing out errors in opposing arguments and provide a comprehensive survey of what we are to understand by the word *everlasting*. There is a really useful Q&A which is not afraid to provide short answers to difficult objections, including "How can God be loving and send people to hell?"

For church members asking questions about hell and its impact on other core beliefs, this would be my go-to book, being shorter and more accessible than the otherwise excellent *Whatever Happened to Hell?* by John Blanchard or *The Great Unknown* by Paul Blackham, both of which are comprehensive surveys. However, of all the responses I have read, I most enjoyed *Hell Under Fire* edited by Christopher Morgan and Robert Peterson. (A shorter version is available – *Is Hell for Real or Does Everyone Go To Heaven?* – but it omits some of the best chapters and so is not as useful as its bigger brother.)

Ed. Christopher W. Morgan & Robert A. Peterson, *Hell Under Fire* (Grand Rapids, Michigan: Zondervan, 2004).

These responses do not, of course, seek to steer a course between the two views outlined above. Rather, they seek to make a case for a traditional understanding, namely ECT, explaining and defending it and – importantly – telling us why it's important. In a characteristically insightful introduction, Al Mohler tells us why this doctrine seems to be open to examination once again. His four reasons are worth repeating.

Hell Under Fire, 37.

First, he argues, we have a changed view of God. Our doctrine of God is under fire, and so it is no surprise that hell itself is under fire, so to speak. Opponents of ECT of all kinds would no doubt agree and argue that it is a fundamental misunderstanding of God that has led us to our erroneous views. So, for example, Stackhouse says "any proper doctrine of hell must take thoroughly into account the goodness of God." He then goes on, however, to set God's holiness against his goodness in making his case. Mohler argues that it is our failure to grasp the exact nature of God that leads to our failings in many other areas.

Four Views, 61.

Second, he says that we have a changed view of justice. This is an important point that Chan and Sprinkle also make clearly. We think of justice in 21st century terms; that is in the category of restorative justice where punishment is designed to bring restoration rather than the ancient concept of retributive justice where no restoration is in view.

Third, he laments the way that a psychological worldview has crept into the church. In particular, this approach seeks to excuse sinful behaviour by explaining it away with reference to circumstances outside of us or out of our control. Whilst true, perhaps this is best included with his fourth point; namely, we have a changed view of sin (and salvation). Sin has become a "lack of self-esteem" and salvation "a liberation from oppression, internal or external."

Hell Under Fire, 40.

Most multi-author books are of mixed quality: this one is no different, although the standard is generally high. There are useful biblical surveys, including those from Doug Moo (on Paul) and Greg Beale (on Revelation). The latter is a particular highlight with Beale, a Revelation specialist, making a compelling argument that all the imagery of Revelation is best interpreted in terms of eternal punishment.

However, the stand out chapter of the book is perhaps Sinclair Ferguson's, entitled "Pastoral theology: the preacher and hell." In it he does an excellent job of what few other books seem to attempt: to apply these truths to the reality of ministry in the local church. Every preacher and pastor should be helped by reading it. For example, responding to Stott's oft-quoted difficulty with ECT ("emotionally, I find the concept intolerable") he says "The emotionally intolerable is also the truth – and therein lies its awfulness." Like Chan and Sprinkle, he offers answers to often-asked questions, including what we should say at funerals of unbelievers and whether hell could ever be considered fair. This book offers no alternative approach, of course. It is unashamedly making a case for ECT without engaging particularly with another view.

Hell Under Fire, 221.

And finally...?

The debate will no doubt roll along, connected as it is to many other doctrines, although it is less visible now than it was ten years ago. In the final analysis, both proponents of the historical view and those who prefer CI seem to be within orthodoxy, although, I would argue, CI is on the fringes of it. Neither camp denies the reality nor the awfulness of sin. Neither camp downgrades evangelism nor diminishes the longing that all people might be saved. Perhaps most significant, explored especially well in *Erasing Hell* and *Hell Under Fire*, is the impact that CI could *potentially* have on other doctrines. For this reason, I remain finally unpersuaded to ditch the traditional understanding.

It is worth reflecting, in conclusion, on some of the lessons we can learn from this debate. Although I have most sympathy and agreement with the traditional ECT position. I cannot say I hold it *comfortably*, as the doctrine is not a comfortable one. We should share our Father's desire to see people saved from hell. However, neither do I want to hold it in the abstract, so this is what I have learnt from reading these (and many other) books on this subject.

1. Christians (and preachers especially) must tremble at hell and rejoice in the salvation we have in Christ. The EA report recounts a time when Francis Schaeffer was asked "for a theological exposition of this matter... [he] instead remained silent and wept." We must preach hell as a dreadful reality (most probably more often than many of us do) alongside the compassion of the Saviour who has himself rescued us from its torment. This debate is much more than an intellectual exercise.

The Nature of Hell, 112.

2. Our preaching and teaching must reflect the regularity of the doctrine of hell in the Scriptures. All of the books surveyed and many more besides make the point clearly that whichever conclusion you come to, you cannot avoid the fact that hell is a key part of the Scriptures and, indeed, without this bad news, the good news has little relevance. One of the strengths of consecutive expository preaching is that it is more likely that the doctrine will be given its biblical prominence. Nor must we be afraid of clear biblical language, avoiding the temptation that a preacher CS Lewis once heard succumbed to when he warned his listeners of "grave eschatological ramifications" if they did not repent.

The Nature of Hell, 112.

3. We must understand the interconnection of doctrines. We cannot consider hell apart from our doctrine of God or humanity or sin or the cross. In other words, we must treasure and teach the value of systematic theology alongside biblical theology (and, we might add, historical and pastoral theology too).

4. Linked to this, we must be wary of maintaining positions which are validated through proof texting. All kinds of positions can be endorsed by finding a verse on which to hang our latest craze. It is important that we take a whole-Bible approach to subjects. It is perfectly true, for example, that verses can be found which seem, in isolation, to support each of the four views in the primary review book. However, even a quick survey of the Bible rules out at least two of these.

5. We have to be clear, based on these approaches, what lies within the realm of orthodoxy and what is outside. I am, as readers will have discerned, finally unpersuaded by the arguments for CI. However, it seems to me that CI does sit within the bounds of orthodoxy, although at the fringes of it. ECT (when compared to CI) is a distinctive doctrine best described as "one to be cherished and retained" rather than one to fall out over. Stott is now in glory, where he has all the answers! I cannot agree with his doctrine of hell. However, like Piper, I would have sat at his feet until the day he died. P

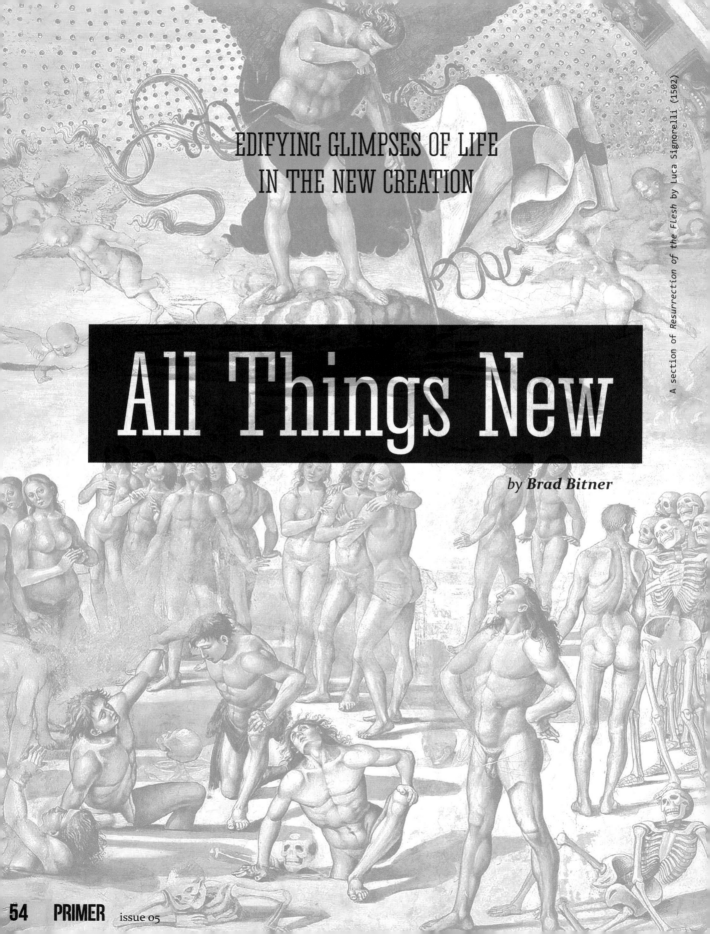

EDIFYING GLIMPSES OF LIFE
IN THE NEW CREATION

All Things New

by *Brad Bitner*

A section of Resurrection of the Flesh by Luca Signorelli (1502)

In the decade before he sailed west in search of Japan and Asia, Christopher Columbus returned repeatedly to several books. One was the *Travels* of Marco Polo. Another was Pierre d'Ailly's *Imago Mundi*. The latter was a kind of encyclopaedia, with maps, figures, calculations and accounts of the habitable zones, peoples, creatures and landscapes of undiscovered shores. Columbus filled the margins of both books with notes recording his hopes, expectations and plans to find a western sea route to these rich, fabled lands. He was hungry for any and every glimpse he might catch of these new worlds. Why? Why did the young explorer expend so much energy piecing together a fragmented image of the Far East? Because he wanted to get there, to *be* there. These glimpses coalesced into an imaginative landscape for Columbus, one that fanned his enthusiasm, focused his energy, sustained his perseverance through failure and guided his preparation to make his voyage finally happen.

Engraving of Christopher Columbus by André Thevet (1584)

As Christians contemplating that far country, the new creation, we find ourselves like Columbus. We are eager to catch glimpses of what life will be like there. Yet, unlike the many fantastic and false reports that reached Columbus, our glimpses come from an utterly sure and sufficient source. In the Bible, God has revealed to us – not *everything* about new creational life – but *everything we need to know* in order that we might live godly and faithful lives as we strain towards that new existence.

This glorious promise is clear: at the end of all things, God will usher in a new heaven and new earth (Rev 21:1-5; Isa 65:17-25). From Genesis to Revelation, from Eden to the New Jerusalem, the grand narrative of God's redemptive work strains towards its climax in the new creation.

For a rich demonstration of God's "eschatological already-not yet new-creational reign" as central to the Bible's storyline, see G. K. Beale, *A New Testament Biblical Theology: The Unfolding of the Old Testament in the New* (Grand Rapids: Baker, 2011).

We catch glimpses of that magnificent promised reality as it is depicted in Scripture. It will be a towering mountain-top (Isa 2:1-4; Rev 21:10), a verdant, royal garden (22:1-2), a luminous city-temple (Rev 21:10-21) in which the people of God feast, dwell and worship in his life-giving glory-presence (Rev 19:9-10; 21:23-24). It will be a stunningly beautiful *meta*-culture – a culture that comes *after* and goes *beyond* present human culture – filled with redeemed people from diverse nations, tribes and languages, all thundering the praise of the Almighty and the Lamb (Rev 14:1-5; 19:1-8; 21:24-26). These glimpses coalesce into an imaginative landscape that is "trustworthy and true" (Rev 21:5; 22:6), one that should fill us with enthusiasm and expectation, and re-orientate us with perseverance and praise even now as we eagerly await this new-creational kingdom come.

Continuity or Discontinuity?

So much is clear in outline. But what will 'ordinary' life in this consummate reality be like? If God is making "all things new", how much – if any – continuity should we expect between our existence here and now and our experience there and then? What will our new bodies be like? Our relationships with family and friends? Moreover, how will the great apocalyptic change, the transition from old to new creation, take place? What does it mean that "earth and sky" will flee from the Lord's presence and there will be "no place for them" (Rev 20:11)? That a fiery cataclysm will overtake the heavens and expose the earth and its works (2 Pet 3:10-12)? Will the works of our hands in this life follow us in some way into the new creation? What will occupy us in the new heaven and earth?

These are not questions of mere curiosity. For we who live in this already-not yet, time between the times, the answers matter precisely because our conception of continuity and/or discontinuity between this life and that to come shapes our priorities and attitudes now. But answering these questions about the 'not yet' is difficult. It is not a matter of grasping one or two biblical passages or truths only. Rather, it requires us to reflect on the teaching of the whole Bible and to take our cues from the unfolding glimpses we are given of new creational existence. As a result, it also requires us to be modest, for we have only glimpses. And exciting as those are, they indicate a reality qualitatively different to and more wonderful than anything we now know or can comprehend. Thus, it should not surprise us that there are differing views amongst Bible-believing, evangelical and (even!) Reformed Christians on these matters.

By way of example, consider the following claims about the biblical teaching on culture in the consummate new creation.

Some, such as Herman Bavinck and Richard Mouw, suggest significant continuity:

All that is true, honourable, just, pure, pleasing, and commendable in the whole of creation, in heaven and on earth, is gathered up in the future city of God – renewed, re-created, boosted to its highest glory.

Herman Bavinck, *Reformed Dogmatics. Volume 4: Holy Spirit, Church, and New Creation.* Edited by John Bolt. Translated by John Vriend (Grand Rapids: Baker, 2008), 720. The entirety of Chapter 18 (The Renewal of Creation), 715-30, is well worth reading.

Richard J. Mouw, *When the Kings Come Marching In: Isaiah and the New Jerusalem* (Grand Rapids: Eerdmans, 1983), 19.

> *[T]he "stuff" of human cultural rebellion will... be gathered into the Holy City... The earth – including the American military and French art and Chinese medicine and Nigerian agriculture – belongs to the Lord. And he will reclaim all of these things, harnessing them for service in the City.*

Others, such as Meredith Kline and David VanDrunen, emphasise discontinuity:

Meredith G. Kline, *Kingdom Prologue: Genesis Foundations for a Covenantal Worldview* (Eugene, OR: Wipf and Stock, 2006), 99. The section is 'Consummation of Glory', 96-101. See further Meredith G. Kline, *God, Heaven and Har Magedon: A Covenantal Tale of Cosmos and Telos* (Eugene, OR: Wipf and Stock, 2006).

> *At the consummation man leaves behind the external culture he has developed through his earthly history... Glorification has made all of this superfluous.*

David VanDrunen, *Living in God's Two Kingdoms: A Biblical Vision for Christianity and Culture* (Wheaton: Crossway, 2010), 66.

> *Our earthly bodies are the only part of the present world that Scripture says will be transformed and taken up into the world-to-come. Believers themselves are the point of continuity between this creation and the new creation. The New Jerusalem is the bride of Christ (Rev 21:2). Asserting that anything else in this world will be transformed and taken up into the world-to-come is speculation beyond Scripture.*

If these theological heavyweights – taking Scripture seriously – can disagree, then it will serve us well to consider why. What are the biblical texts and biblical-theological assumptions and arguments that underlie these claims? When coming to the same verses and issues, why do some tend towards continuity and others towards discontinuity? While we do not have space here to consider every relevant text and assumption, the following sections touch on some of the key passages and discernible emphases in the debates.

Spiritual Bodies and Relationships

One thing absolutely clear in Scripture is the continuity of believers themselves from the old to the new creation. Yet even here, we are confronted with a wonderful and radical change wrought by God's resurrection power: Jesus Christ was raised from the dead as the "firstfruits" of the new creation (1 Cor 15:20; see also Col 1:15-20). And all who are "in Christ" by faith have already become new creations (2 Cor 5:17), being spiritually transformed by the Spirit of Christ. This is true now in part – we are *being* transformed (1 Cor 3:18) and one day will be true in full when believers are glorified with resurrection *bodies* (1 Thess 4:15-17; 1 Cor 15:51-53; 2 Cor 5:1-5; Phil 3:20-21). Newly embodied, we will be perfectly suited to our glorious new environment and, most importantly, for the glorious presence of our God. These will be resurrected bodies, re-formed by the Spirit. As Augustine rightly notes, "The bodies of the just will be spiritual after the resurrection, not because they will cease to be bodies but because they will live by the vivifying Spirit."

City of God 13.22

"But someone will ask, 'How are the dead raised? With what kind of body will they come?'" (1 Cor 15:35). To the sceptic, Paul's original answer still stands as a rebuke: "How foolish!"(1 Cor 15:36). For the believer, however, what Paul goes on to teach in that passage has inspired a variety of conceptions of resurrection bodies in church history. Luca Signorelli's 1502 painting 'Resurrection of the Flesh,' is one attempt to capture the moment proclaimed by the Apostle a few verses later in 1 Cor 15:51-52:

1 Cor 15:51-52

> *Listen, I tell you a mystery: We will not all sleep, but we will all be changed – in a flash, in the twinkling of an eye, at the last trumpet. For the trumpet will sound, the dead will be raised imperishable, and we will be changed.*

In Signorelli's fresco, a pair of angels hover overhead, blowing blasts upon long trumpets while below the dead struggle to emerge from a featureless earth as if from desert quicksand. Some are skeletons, not yet fully clothed incorruptibly; others stand, newly enfleshed with rippled Renaissance physiques, embracing as if reunited with old friends.

Although reflecting his late medieval time and place in the lack of ethnic diversity, Signorelli's depiction rightly highlights the new *body* as a centrepiece of the new creation. We know from elsewhere in the Bible (e.g.

Resurrection of the Flesh by Luca Signorelli (1502)

Dan 12:2; John 5:28-29) that *all* will be raised, some to judgment and some to new life, according to their faith in Christ. Several New Testament texts and themes related to the resurrection bodies of believers are worth dwelling on briefly.

In 1 Thess 4:13-18, we glimpse the extraordinary event Signorelli laboured to depict. Thessalonian believers are grieving for fellow Christians who have died (4:13). But Paul exhorts them to have hope and find comfort in the certainty of resurrection. The foundational presupposition is that Jesus died and rose again. And so also will it be for those of his people who die; God will raise them in the same way (4:14). With a sudden, sonic burst reminiscent of the thunderous noise and trumpet blast on Sinai (Exod 19:16-20), Jesus will appear from the heavens (4:16). And at his appearing believers dead and alive will soar into the atmosphere to meet him. Just like children joyfully pouring out the door and running through the garden gate to greet mum or dad returning home after an absence, some sprinting ahead and others following behind, so Paul says those living at the moment of Christ's return will by no means overtake (NIV: *precede*) those rising from their graves (4:15). The dead are raised; then the living are 'caught up' (4:16). This language of being caught up, snatched or transported points to the powerful, supernatural action of the Spirit (see Acts 8:39). With transformed bodies capable of astonishing mobility, we will eagerly rush to meet our Lord, forever to remain with him (4:17). With these words and this reality, Paul says, encourage one another (4:18)! As Christians, we should contemplate more prayerfully this glimpse of the inaugural moment of the consummation. As Bible teachers we should use it to stir up a godly anticipation in our people. The thought of meeting and remaining forever with Christ in resurrected bodies ought to fill our hearts with comfort and hope as we suffer the deaths of beloved, believing family and friends. And it should infuse us with eagerness for the wonder and joy of that day.

In 1 Cor 15:35-49 we catch further glimpses of the spiritual bodies that await believers. Death is not the end (and nihilism is not therefore an option); neither rotting flesh nor dry bones in the grave pose a barrier to the power of Christ. Just as a seed 'dies' before sprouting, so our bodies will be re-made according to God's design (15:36-41). From 15:42-49, with a series of contrasts, Paul sketches for us the qualitatively different beauty of those new bodies: not perishable, but imperishable; not dishonourable, but glorious; not characterised by weakness, but by power; not natural, but spiritual; not earthly, but heavenly; not mortal, but immortal. There are, Paul reminds us, two Adams and two creations. And by extension there are two kinds of human bodies (or *images*, 15:49) corresponding to those Adams and their respective creations. Jesus, the last Adam, has – by his resurrection, and especially on the basis of his ascension and exaltation – become a *life-giving Spirit* (15:45). Only he is able to transform us into perfected versions of ourselves that can enter into the life of the new creational kingdom he has won for us as an inheritance (15:50).

Thus, we see that we will have new, glorious, *spiritual* bodies. Of what substance or material – who can tell? Only we know that we will be subject neither to decay nor sinful desire. Here we find there is substantial *discontinuity* between this life and the next. Our new bodies will never weaken or wear out, never grow ill, never succumb to stress, never be destroyed. But more importantly than how precisely we will appear (will I be resurrected as the eighteen year old me? the forty-one year old me? the me at the time of my death? the clean-shaven or the bearded me?) is that *I will be the sanctified me*. My personality perfected. My memories, my manner, my affections and desires – all will be me, but me transformed and holy. What a hope! There is much we still don't know about this. As 1 John 3:2 says, "what we will be has not yet been made known. But we know that when Christ appears, we shall be like him, for we shall see him as he is." It continues, prodding us, by the Spirit's power, to strive for holiness *now*. "All who have this hope in him purify themselves, just as he is pure" (1 John 3:3).

There is more we could say about our glorified spiritual bodies. What implications are there for the way I use my body now (à la 1 Cor 6:19-20)? What about the glorified bodies of God's children with disabilities of various kinds? These are questions deserving careful thought beyond the space we have here. But it is important to highlight some interpretative considerations that must guide us. To begin with, many rightly draw inferences on the basis of Christ's resurrection body. For example, we know that the resurrected Jesus entered closed and locked rooms (John 20:19, 26); he vanished from sight suddenly (Luke 24:31); he ate bread and fish (Luke 24:30, 42-43; John 21:9-14); his resurrected body still bore the *stigmata*, the wounds of his crucifixion (John 21:27). Surely these truths must inform our thinking about new creational life.

Yet we must also ponder what else the Bible reveals about resurrection bodies and seek to construct a coherent biblical-theological doctrine that accounts for all the texts. Take, for example, the fact that the risen Jesus ate fish. Surely this implies we will similarly eat and drink in the new creation. But two thoughts give us pause as we consider what it might mean to eat and drink in the new heavens and earth. First, the Gospel accounts of Jesus' post-resurrection body are, quite obviously, pre-ascension and involve his action within this old creation. Furthermore, we have other biblical texts to consider. 1 Corinthians 6:13, for example, likely affirms that God will 'destroy' both stomachs and food. What can this mean for our spiritual bodies in the new creation? Fee argues that "both food and the stomach belong to the present age," linking this to 1 Cor 15:42-49, and arguing that "such a *pneumatic* (spiritual) body has no need for [this worldly] stomach and food." But how do we bring together the teaching of 1 Cor 6:13; 15:42-49; and texts like Luke 24:43? Will we have new digestive systems and processes that are somehow qualitatively different? Will we enjoy new creational food but without the same need for sustenance? According to Turretin, "Although the organic parts ought not any longer to survive for *use* and *operation* [so 1 Cor 6:13], still they will survive for *integrity* and *ornament*." His stress on integrity is important. We see that the precise *form* or *material* of our body is less important than the continuity and transformation of our *identity* as whole, spiritual persons in the new creation: "The bottom line is that the sorts of changes which make one fit to be a citizen of heaven need not destroy one's personal identity." In our spiritual bodies, we will be recognisably us, but we will be us *perfected*.

Paul uses the same word here (*katargeo*) as in 1 Cor 15:24 where death is destroyed.

Gordon D. Fee, *1 Corinthians* (Grand Rapids: Eerdmans, 1987), 255. For 6:13 in the larger flow of argument, see 253-57.

Francis Turretin, *Institutes of Elenctic Theology, Volume Three: Eighteenth through Twentieth Topics*. Edited by James T. Dennison; Translated by George Musgrave Giger (Phillipsburg, NJ: P&R, 1997), 574, emphasis mine.

Katherin A Rogers, "Anselmian Meditations on Heaven" in *Paradise Understood: New Philosophical Essays about Heaven*. Edited by T. Ryan Byerly and Eric J. Silverman (Oxford: OUP, 2017), 37.

More from Turretin

In his 'Twentieth Topic: The Last Things', Q. 2 (571-74), Turretin emphasises the transformed continuity of our new creational identities from a number of angles: In the first place, *re*-surrection assumes that there is a person to be raised to new life. As Jesus says to the disciples in Luke 24:39, "It is I myself!" We do not expect to be created *ex nihilo* (in which case we wouldn't be quite ourselves); rather, we will be *newly* made. Moreover, this is true for those who do not trust in Christ in this life as well. For God's justice to be just, those resurrected unto judgment must be the same sinners who deserve that judgment. Further, even in the flow of 1 Cor 15, Paul insists that believers' new spiritual selves are significantly continuous with their dusty, perishable old creation selves. We might miss the emphasis in some of our translations, but 1 Cor 15:53 reads, "For it is necessary that *this* perishable [body] clothe itself with imperishability and *this* mortal [body] clothe itself with immortality." Likewise in Philippians 3:21, the transformation of our lowly bodies to be like Jesus's risen body clearly involves the same subject. It is *we* who are transformed (the verb signifies *renovation* or *reconstruction*).

Geerhardus Vos, *Reformed Dogmatics, Volume Five: Ecclesiology, The Means of Grace, Eschatology* (Grand Rapids: Lexham Press, 2016), 274.

In all this, we must "be modest... and not wise beyond what is taught in Scripture." Yet even with these modest conclusions we see implications and expectations for our new creational existence as well as for life now. When we consider our relationships in the new creation we must not miss the fact that our notion of family will be reconfigured. We need to resist an individualistic conception of resurrected life. Certainly we will enjoy renewed fellowship with believing parents, spouses, and children. But our family will expand – massively. The entire community of the redeemed through time and space will form our new creational family. This ought to give us pause as we 'do' church in the present age. Our spiritual bonds with brothers and sisters in Christ are, in the end, more enduring than ties of blood and birth. So everything in the here and now – our embrace of our new family in the church, our love and hospitality, our service and care for fellow believers – is cast in the glory-light of the wedding festival of the Lamb in the age to come.

Annihilation or Renewal?

"Some say the world will in end in fire / some say in ice," wrote the poet Robert Frost. The Bible affirms fire. But will it be an annihilating or renovating fire? Will it result in the utter destruction or purification of this creation? Traditionally Lutheran theologians have tended to think in terms of old substance destroyed and the creation of new substance as God brings into being the glorified world. Reformed theologians have generally thought of substance preserved, restored, or purified.

Vos, *Reformed Dogmatics, Volume 5*, 308.

2 Peter 3:7-13 is one of the key texts and it is difficult. At first glance, much is clear. We see an apocalyptic vision of the great change. In the context of the letter, its point is to serve as a reminder that stirs in us repentance, holiness and a patient expectation in view of the end which is really a new beginning (3:1, 9, 11-12). A blazing end awaits this old creation (3:7, 12). In keeping with the Old Testament motif of the Day of the Lord, it is the flames of judgment that will expose the works done on this earth (3:10).

But a careful exegesis uncovers much that is not as clear as we might first assume. Of 3:10 alone, Doug Moo has written, "Each of these clauses presents problems of translation and interpretation, with the difficulties increasing as we move through them." These puzzle pieces can also be put together in several combinations to generate quite different conclusions about what is to come.

Douglas J. Moo, *2 Peter and Jude*. NIV Application Commentary (Grand Rapids: Zondervan, 1996), 189.

If, for example, we think 3:10 teaches the fiery annihilation of this world in its entirety – understanding the Greek word *stoicheia* as 'elements' and taking that to embrace the very sub-atomic building blocks of the universe – then we will be led to a strongly discontinuous view. The implication would be that this earth and its human culture and artefacts will perish. Moreover, we will be prompted to read other biblical texts in light of these constraints from 2 Pet 3. If, however, we understand 3:10 to focus on an apocalyptic unveiling, a 'peeling back' of the heavens – then we might have the 'heavenly bodies' (*stoicheia* could also refer to them) being burned up, while the earth is 'laid bare' in a judicial sense (the verb Peter uses, *heuresthēsetai*, can mean that). If that is right, then at the very least we cannot rule out a reading that embraces more continuity. The fire may destroy the heavens (3:10) while renewing or purifying the earth (3:7). As Bauckham contends, it is less "the dissolution of the earth than the judgment of humanity" which is in view here. The latter interpretation must still account for the "everything will be destroyed" (NIV) of 3:11 and the *stoicheia* melting in 3:12. The annihilation reading must reckon with the other biblical texts pointing to radical change but not obliteration (e.g., Heb 12:26-29; Ps 102:26-27, which is also quoted in Heb 1:10-12). Vos notes, "If annihilation is assumed, then texts that speak of change are absolutely impossible to explain. If change is assumed, the texts that seem to speak of annihilation can still be explained in a very sound sense."

Richard J. Bauckham, *Jude, 2 Peter*. Word Biblical Commentary, 50 (Waco, TX: Word, 1983), 324.

Vos, *Reformed Dogmatics, Volume 5*, 309.

A brief look at the larger context in 2 Pet 3 reveals more. The redemptive-historical model for the great conflagration is the flood of Noah's day: "the world of that time was deluged and destroyed" (3:6). Note several things here. The pre-flood creation is referred to as "the world of that time" (lit. 'the *then* world') in contrast to "the present heavens and earth" (3:7; lit. 'the *now* heavens and earth'). The divine word of deluge-judgment marked a hiatus between two worlds. Yet it was not an annihilation of all created matter. It was a thoroughgoing, destruction of all humanity, including its violent culture and technologies. Yet there was continuity amidst significant discontinuity. As the flood waters receded to reveal the ancient mountains and valleys, those who were saved from the cataclysm in the ark emerged into a new world. We should not forget that this is the contextually signalled paradigm for final judgment in 2 Peter's scorching eschatological vision. At the very least, then, it would not appear to be the case that this text rules out all continuity. The change will certainly be radical. But the fire is likely to be purifying and not wholly annihilating.

Bavinck, *Reformed Dogmatics. Volume 4*, 717.

This leads us to the question of the works of our hands, the residue of human cultures in this age. The gardens we cultivate, the books we write, the machines we build, the art we create – will these things be renewed? Will they find some place in the heavenly meta-culture? Many follow Richard Mouw in looking to Isaiah 65:17-25 for specific signs of transformed cultural continuity. But questions arise concerning Mouw's handling of the figurative language and biblical-theological deployment of that beautiful passage. Others see in 1 Corinthians 15:58 or Revelation 11:15, 14:13 or 21:24 indications of a renewed or transformed cultural continuity. Each of these texts must be examined carefully in context, but none seems to require or reveal a specific and stable cultural carryover.

On 'labour' in 1 Cor 15:58 as gospel ministry see Peter Orr, "Abounding in the Work of the Lord (1 Cor 15:58): Everything We Do as Christians or Specific Gospel Work?" *Themelios* 38.2 (2013), 205-14. On a negative evaluation of each of these Revelation texts with respect to cultural continuity, see G. K. Beale, *The Book of Revelation* (Grand Rapids: Eerdmans, 1999). Beale speaks repeatedly of the "qualitatively different" character of new creational culture.

It seems then, that there are very few texts which indicate with exegetical clarity a specific new creational role for our old creation material culture. In terms of biblical theology and doctrine, the principles of resurrection, restoration and renewal are suggestive. But in the end we should remain agnostic about particulars. Or else we speculate. Lovely storied accounts, such as the gift of Niggle's leaf and Narnia's dimensions cascading "further up and further in" are often brought to bear in this debate. Yet they remain sanctified speculation rooted in a holy hope of transformed continuity.

Many evangelical and Reformed accounts refer to these stories: J. R. R. Tolkien, "Leaf by Niggle" in *Tree and Leaf* (London: Unwin, 1964), 73-92; C. S. Lewis, *The Last Battle* (London: Bodley Head, 1959).

It is important to note that robust doctrines of creation and vocation will prevent us from minimising the work of our hands to the glory of God (1 Cor 10:31; Col 3:17). These provide us with other biblical means by which to value our work and activity in this broken but beautiful world. We might also ask ourselves why we long for our cultural work to follow us into the new earth? Is it the glory of God, king of all creation (old and new), or of his image-bearers that we have chiefly in mind? Do we trust in our loving, all-wise, all-creative Triune God? He will provide for us not only perfect spiritual bodies but also a Spirit-wrought setting, a garden-city of surpassing beauty in which to engage in our primary new creational service, namely, to worship him.

Sixty Sabbaths and More

Finally, we should realise that, in biblical terms, new creational life is Sabbatical life. In Eden Adam was meant to enter into the Sabbath rest of God's enthronement if he faithfully guarded and kept the holy beauty of the garden (Gen 2:1-3, 15). That Sabbath escalation was to have been, for Yahweh's vice-regent, an entrance into glory, with all creation following in his train. It was a story intended, from the beginning, to move from creation to new creation by means of a transformed continuity and escalation. But Adam failed. He, and his children in him, sinned and fell short of the consummation-glory.

In response, the Lord of glory, resting from his initial work of creation, has remained in his Sabbath day (Heb 4:10). Paradoxically, he is still working away within the old creation in order to birth the new (John 5:17). Thus, there yet remains a Sabbath rest for God's people (Heb 4:9). But this will be a Sabbath rest of great and holy activity, not of "blessed inaction." Life in the glorious new earth will overflow with joy celebrated by the assembly of the firstborn and innumerable angels encircling the heavenly Mt. Zion (Heb 12:22-23). After a great shaking loose from sin and death and all that is unclean, we will eternally keep Sabbath in that unshakeable new creational kingdom (Heb 12:26-29).

Bavinck, *Reformed Dogmatics, Volume 4*, 727.

Such a redemptive-historical vision of life in a new age of unending Sabbath should challenge us in our worship in this present age. If worship is an in-breaking of that future lively rest – and especially so on the Lord's Day – then perhaps we ought to approach our worship (and the day) with far more joy and expectancy.

There is a section of the Jewish Talmud (*Gemara*, *Berakhot* 57b), a commentary on rabbinic interpretation of the Old Testament, that alludes to the Jewish delight in the Sabbath. It claims that the Sabbath is merely one-sixtieth, the slightest foretaste, of the world to come. In other words, the new heavens and new earth is sixty Sabbaths and more! How much more, as Christians resting in the finished work of Messiah Jesus, should we rejoice on the Lord's Day? With prayer and praise we assemble as God's people, ushered to his very throne. We should be energised by focusing our hearts, minds and bodies on aspects of that glorious existence which awaits those of us in Christ. Delighting in the in-breaking Sabbath *now* can whet our appetites for the new Sabbatical world to come. As G. K. Beale notes, "Churches should be reminded that the scenes of heavenly worship [in Revelation] are to be the model for our earthly worship every Lord's Day." With this in mind, like Columbus, we too may find ourselves increasingly eager to *be* there, increasingly sustained in our perseverance through suffering, inspired toward diligence in our callings and delight in this creation. And on that great day when all things are new, theology will finally and fully merge into doxology and our praise now will be our praise then, only transformed and amplified. And all will be glory! P

G. K. Beale with David H. Campbell, *Revelation, Shorter Commentary* (Grand Rapids: Eerdmans, 2015), 32.

PULLING BACK THE CURTAIN

A PREACHER'S GUIDE TO
REVELATION by
GRAHAM BEYNON

The classic Star Trek line – "to boldly go where no man has gone before" – was actually used by a senior minister about me. We'd just finished preaching Revelation chapters 1-3 which had been shared amongst a number of preachers at our church. I was about to embark on

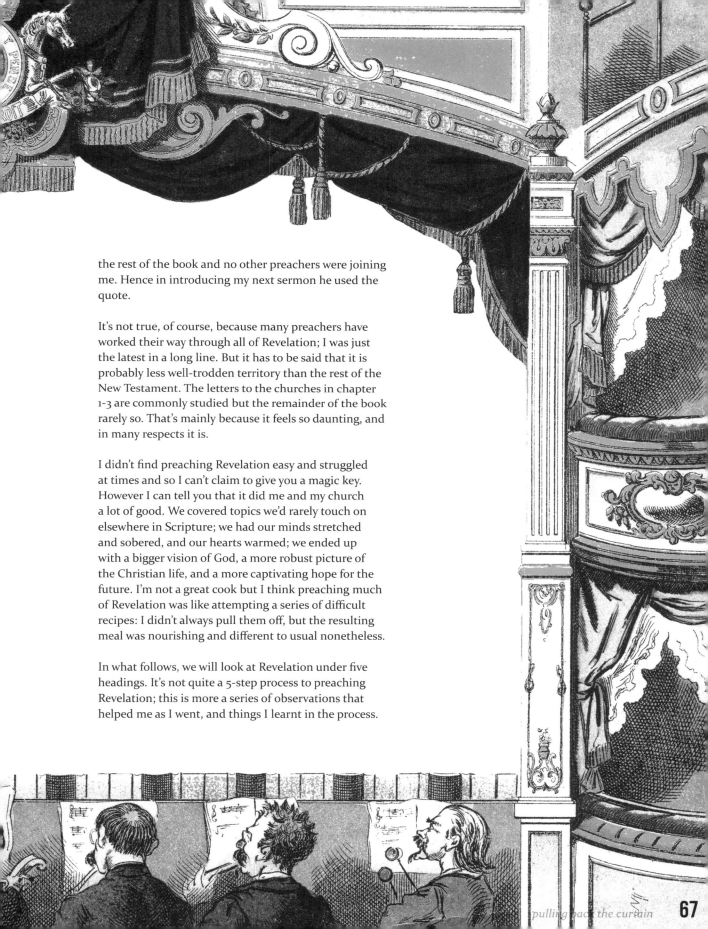

the rest of the book and no other preachers were joining me. Hence in introducing my next sermon he used the quote.

It's not true, of course, because many preachers have worked their way through all of Revelation; I was just the latest in a long line. But it has to be said that it is probably less well-trodden territory than the rest of the New Testament. The letters to the churches in chapter 1-3 are commonly studied but the remainder of the book rarely so. That's mainly because it feels so daunting, and in many respects it is.

I didn't find preaching Revelation easy and struggled at times and so I can't claim to give you a magic key. However I can tell you that it did me and my church a lot of good. We covered topics we'd rarely touch on elsewhere in Scripture; we had our minds stretched and sobered, and our hearts warmed; we ended up with a bigger vision of God, a more robust picture of the Christian life, and a more captivating hope for the future. I'm not a great cook but I think preaching much of Revelation was like attempting a series of difficult recipes: I didn't always pull them off, but the resulting meal was nourishing and different to usual nonetheless.

In what follows, we will look at Revelation under five headings. It's not quite a 5-step process to preaching Revelation; this is more a series of observations that helped me as I went, and things I learnt in the process.

APPRECIATE THE GENRE

Revelation calls itself a "prophecy" (1:3) and it contains elements of being a letter. However, it most clearly belongs to the *apocalyptic* genre. Apocalyptic literature (from the Greek for 'revelation' or 'revealing') is often marked by the presence of supernatural beings (e.g. angels), symbolic pictures (e.g. lampstands), and numerology (the significance of numbers). Common themes in apocalyptic literature include the suffering of God's people, the battle between God and evil, and God's final victory over all enemies. However what is more foundational is the idea of 'revelation': that is the drawing back of the curtain on reality. Apocalyptic texts invite us to view the world a different way and to see greater cosmic significance in our lives. As we preach Revelation then, while the genre can feel alien, there can and should be a sense of 'privilege' – we're getting to look behind the curtain, we're seeing a new perspective on reality.

Apocalyptic literature usually involves imagery, where what is *seen* is foundational to what is being revealed (in contrast to prophecy which usually focuses on what is *heard*). We are alerted to this in the opening verses where Jesus 'makes known' what must take place to John. The Greek word used means he 'signified' it, which points to imagery, confirmed by the use of 'show' in verse 1.

In the next verse we're told that John testifies to 'everything he saw – that is the word of God and the testimony of Jesus' (1:2). So what comes is the word of God, but John 'saw' it. It came in picture language. To put it differently, Revelation is an audio-visual display that John is relating, and it is the visual element that is dominant. The emphasis on what John sees is repeated through the book (see, for example 1:19, and the section on structure below).

The use of symbolism means we should not take descriptions literally. For example when Jesus places his right hand on John (1:17), we don't have to ask what he has done with the stars he was previously holding (1:16). Or when John sees a lamb standing in the centre of the throne (5:6) we don't need to ask what's happened to the one sitting on the throne (5:1). You probably didn't even think of those questions, which shows you are instinctively reading this as symbolic rather than literal language.

This means that attempts to draw what is described are rarely helpful. The symbolic pictures have a dream-like quality such that they can change and morph, often holding more than one meaning at once. For example, in chapter 21, how would you draw the New Jerusalem? It is given the dimensions of a cube while still having gates and foundations. It is as clear as crystal while being made of gold, and is a city while also wearing a wedding dress. You aren't supposed to draw it as an entity – which requires thinking of it in literal terms – but rather allow each part of the symbolism to convey its own truth.

There are then a number of special features of how Revelation is written. For example, John often hears something said, and then he looks and sees something else – but the words and the vision go together. So in chapter 5 he hears that the lion of the tribe of Judah has triumphed. The next line is 'And I saw'. But what John sees is a lamb looking as if it had been slain. The words and vision go together, so the slain lamb is the victorious lion.

That example is relatively well known but the same pattern is true elsewhere. For example, in chapter 7 John 'hears' the number of those who were sealed (a symbol of salvation), which is reported audibly as 144,000, 12,000 from each tribe (7:4-8). Then he 'looks' and sees a 'great multitude that no one could count from every nation, tribe, people and language' (7:9). So the 144,000 (standing for the complete people of God) is the vast multitude of those who are saved.

Other examples are seen in 17:1-6 and 21:9-10. This pattern can be also reversed where John sees something first and then hears – for example 6:1-2 and 14:1-5.

A last word on numbers: they are symbolic! Seven is the number of completeness or perfection; four is created completeness (e.g. four corners of the earth). There are then combinations such as the fourfold formula, 'tribe, tongue, people and nation' being used seven times in the book. Names or descriptions of God and Jesus also occur in startlingly precise numbers (combinations of four and seven).

Twelve represents the people of God, as does its multiple in 144 (and its larger versions like 144,000). This is of significance in the vision of the New Jerusalem because the dimensions of the walls are 144 cubits thick and the city is 12,000 by 12,000 stadia. The city then does not so much represent the place of the new creation as the people of God – which is why it is also called 'the bride, the wife of the Lamb'.

The number 3½ is common in apocalyptic literature for a period of suffering. We should know it from Daniel where we have the repeated refrain of 'time, times and half a time,' i.e. 1, 2 and ½. It comes in Revelation 11 and 12 in reference to 3½ days, 42 months (which is 3½ years) and 1,260 days (also 3½ years based on 360 days per annum). Commentaries should be your friend in guiding you through this (and I make some recommendations at the end of the article) but read carefully yourself.

GET YOUR HEAD ROUND THE STRUCTURE

Revelation feels fairly structured at the start – there's a prologue and the opening vision of Jesus, followed by the letters to the churches. We might pick up some structural details such as each letter involves a description of Jesus from chapter 1 and a call to 'hear' and to be 'victorious'.

Chapters 4 and 5 can also feel okay – they picture God the Father and then the Lord Jesus – but once we're in chapter 6 and beyond it is all trumpets, bowls, and beasts and we very easily feel lost. What feels like chaos, however, is actually a highly structured book and the structure really helps in knowing what is going on.

There is first a macro-structure which is framed by a pattern of invitation to John to come and be shown something new and the repeated mention of being 'in the Spirit':

Rev 4:1-2

> *After this I looked, and there before me was a door standing open in heaven. And the voice I had first heard speaking to me like a trumpet said, 'Come up here, and I will show you what must take place after this.' At once I was in the Spirit...*

Rev 17:1,3

> *One of the seven angels who had the seven bowls came and said to me, 'Come, I will show you the punishment of the great prostitute, who sits by many waters...' Then the angel carried me away in the Spirit...*

Rev 21:9-10

> *One of the seven angels who had the seven bowls full of the seven last plagues came and said to me, 'Come, I will show you the bride, the wife of the Lamb.' And he carried me away in the Spirit...*

We should also note the one other use of 'in the Spirit' which begins the first vision in chapter 1:

Rev 1:10

> *On the Lord's Day I was in the Spirit, and I heard behind me a loud voice like a trumpet...*

These verses, plus some observations below, give the following divisions:

The section labelled 'Transition' above does not have its own marker phrase. However it clearly acts as a transition between the two parallel sections 4 and 6. The similarity of sections 4 and 6 are seen both by the repetition of their start (the same angel saying, 'Come and I will show you...') but also by their similar conclusion, both of which involve comment from this angel and reprimand of John for wrong worship (see 19:9-10 and 22:6-11). The transition section has its own clear unity as it consists of a series of seven visions (the magic number in Revelation), all introduced identically ('And I saw...').

This structure already has implications for preaching. For example it is common to preach 21:1-8 with 21:9 onwards because it is all describing the New Jerusalem. However the structural markers – as well as a close reading of the text – show that this description starts afresh in 21:9, while 21:1-8 is the last of the seven visions in section 5.

Within section 3, the main body of the book (chapters 4-16), there is a detailed micro-structure. It divides first into chapters 4-5 which contain the visions of God the Father and the Lamb. Chapters 6-16 then involve three series of seven (seals, trumpets and bowls). There is a repeated but escalating formula which begins in the first section (4:5) and then occurs at the end of each of the series of seven.

4:5   *lightning, sounds, thunder*
8:5   *lightning, sounds, thunder, earthquake*
11:19   *lightning, sounds, thunder, earthquake, hail storm*
16:18   *lightning, sounds, thunder, severe earthquake, huge hail storm*

This shows us that all of the judgments of chapters 6-16 are grounded in the vision of chapters 4-5. This is emphasised too by the fact that the first series of seven (the seals) are connected to the scroll of chapter 5 (see 6:1ff).

This observation on structure reveals the key to how Revelation is written. Each of the series of seven (seals, bowls and trumpets) end with the same, but escalating, picture of judgment. This is usually understood as giving us repeated pictures of the same event in increasing detail. It is as if we arrive at the same moment several times but are approaching it from an increasingly close viewpoint. This counters the idea that Revelation is basically linear or chronological. Rather it suggests that 'the end' is reached several times, and we're being given repeated viewing of the same story.

I usually illustrate this by asking where God promises to wipe away every tear. Most people answer that it's somewhere towards the end of the book (21:4 to be precise). I agree and then read from chapter 7, 'And God will wipe away every tear from their eyes' (7:17). So at the end of chapter 7 we have reached 'the end' – God is dwelling with his people and wiping away their tears. And yet the book carries on because we then cover the same story again, and again. This is sometimes called the 'recapitulation' view. It means that in preaching much of chapters 6-16 we know we will cover the same territory but from a new angle and so with something new to say.

Within the series of seven seals, bowls and trumpets come the last pieces of structural complexity. There are interludes between the sixth and seventh seals (7:1-17) and the sixth and seventh trumpets (10:1-11:14). There is no such interlude in the series of bowls – the climatic end comes quickly. Lastly, chapters 12-14 sit between the end of the trumpets and the start of the bowls. This section is of great significance in understanding the message of the book: it covers the work of Jesus, the persecution of the church by Satan through the beast, the proclamation of the gospel, and the final eschatological harvest.

Having got some handle on the structure, the detail can come as you move through the text. The key is to know that it is highly structured, and repetitive.

KNOW THE OLD TESTAMENT REALLY WELL

The first person who taught me Revelation said there were two clues to understanding it: first, to read it lots of times; and second, to know the Old Testament really well. He spoke with wisdom.

This depends on when one thinks an allusion becomes an actual quote.

The Old Testament is rarely, if ever, actually quoted in Revelation. But the subsequent lack of footnotes at the bottom of the Bible page is misleading; in reality barely a few verses go by without an Old Testament connection. It is commonly recognised that Revelation contains more Old Testament references than any other New Testament book.

A few examples will illustrate. The opening verses of chapter 1 are patterned on Daniel chapter 2 (see Dan 2:28-30 and 45-47) with the repetition of revealing (or showing) the 'things that must take place'. There are many other connections between Daniel and Revelation and so the similarity at the start makes sense. Chapter 13 has the beast out of the sea which is an amalgamation of the first three beasts of Daniel 7, but with the characteristics of the fourth beast, especially its boastful words and war against God's people. Daniel appears in other sections as well.

Zechariah, and especially chapter 4, is also commonly referenced. Chapter 4 includes:

> - *A lampstand with seven lamps – see Revelation 4:5*
> - *The seven eyes of the Lord – see Revelation 1:4 and 5:6*
> - *The two olive trees – see Revelation 11:3-4*

Exodus is also foundational, with Jesus as the Passover Lamb who is slain to redeem his people and make them a kingdom of priests to serve God (chapter 5). The people of God are pictured as singing the song of Moses (from Exodus 15) in Revelation 15. In addition, the judgments of God are modelled on the plagues of Egypt.

Other key Old Testament books are Isaiah, Ezekiel, and Psalms. We mentioned the well-known phrase where God wipes away our tears (used in Revelation 7 and 21), which originates in Isaiah 25:8, as well as the better known 'new heaven and earth' texts from Isaiah 65.

The prevalence of Old Testament imagery shows that Revelation sees itself as both repeating and fulfilling earlier Scripture. An example of repetition would be connections with Daniel showing a similar need to persevere under severe persecution, knowing faithfulness is always rewarded. An example of fulfilment would be the connections with Exodus showing that through Jesus comes God's true redemption and final acts of judgment. It is the second category that dominates and there is a gathering together of Old Testament texts, giving them their final fulfilled meaning. Hence Revelation represents what Richard Bauckham has helpfully called "the climax of prophecy."

See Richard Bauckham, *The Climax of Prophecy: Studies on the Book of Revelation* (London: T&T Clark, 1998).

This means that Revelation fulfils many biblical-theological themes such as temple, kingship and judgment. This is most pronounced in the closing scenes which draw together Ezekiel's vision of a new temple with the garden-temple of Eden, along with eschatological fulfilment of promises in Isaiah of safety and security. On top of this comes fulfilment of the covenant promise of relationship with God ('they will see his face and his name will be on their foreheads' 22:4), the end of the curse, and reigning with Christ. Such passages are high points both in the truth they depict and also the drawing together of the previous biblical storyline.

Preaching Revelation, then, will involve constant Old Testament study. Of course we don't all know the Old Testament as well as we'd like, so helpful aids include commentaries, study Bibles, lists of allusions and verbal parallels (such as published by the United Bible Society's edition of the Greek New Testament) and Carson and Beale's *Commentary on the New Testament Use of the Old Testament* (Nottingham: IVP, 2006).

This is one of the great enriching factors in preaching Revelation, both for the preacher and the listeners. Naturally, not all cross-references can be mentioned, let alone explained, or a sermon will quickly become tiresome. But judicious use of the Old Testament background will encourage listeners in appreciating the depth and richness of Revelation itself, but also the continuity and fulfilment of the Bible's storyline.

DECIDE ON YOUR FUNDAMENTAL APPROACH

Approaches to Revelation are usually divided into four, however they are not watertight categories and one can adopt more than one of them at a time. The usual descriptions are as follows. To help with comparison I'll illustrate using the same passage in Revelation (Rev 13) for each one.

PRETERIST

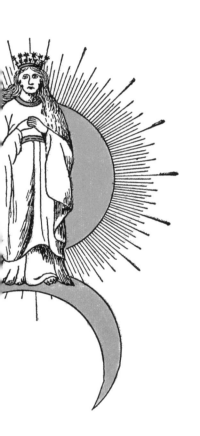

From the Latin word *praeter* meaning 'past', this approach sees the fulfilment of most, or all, of the book within the first century A.D. It takes very seriously the opening words that 'the time is near' (1:3) and 'I am coming soon' (22:20). In particular, the impending judgment is seen as being fulfilled in the Roman destruction of Jerusalem in A.D. 70 (although another form sees it as the destruction of the Roman Empire in the 5th century).

So for example the persecution of chapter 13 is describing the actual persecution in the first century including restrictions on buying and selling (13:16-17). This is usually related to the Emperor Cult in the Roman Empire. The number of the beast is taken to represent Nero (through letters having numeric value) and it is expected that Christians living at the time would have known that.

This view has more going for it than is often thought. It takes seriously the immediacy of application to the original hearers assuming that they would recognise what was being described and fulfilled.

However there are two weaknesses. First it can end up studying Revelation as an already-fulfilled book, whereas I would say that one of the points of apocalyptic literature is to lift specific examples out of their historical confines to represent them as ongoing truths. So chapter 13 teaches that God's people will continue to be persecuted by corrupt political powers – it doesn't only apply to the first century. Some preterist interpreters acknowledge this and so their position can start to combine with the 'idealist' below.

Secondly, and more significantly, preterist interpretations see the final judgment and arrival of the 'New Jerusalem' as fulfilled in the condemnation of Israel in A.D. 70 and the 'arrival' of the church. To my mind this 'complete fulfilment' view does not do justice to the details of the text.

FUTURIST

This is the opposite of the preterist position in seeing virtually all of Revelation as predicting future events close to the second coming of Christ. This is usually taken to be true from chapter 4 onwards. Futurist approaches are often connected to various dispensational views with associated events such as the 'Rapture' and the 'Great Tribulation'. Particular interpretations vary between *classic* and *progressive* dispensationalism. Progressive dispensationalism sees some fulfilment in the first century, but only partial; they may also see some sections of Revelation (e.g. chapters 4-5) as describing current truths rather than being future. Classic dispensationalism tends to read everything as lying in the future with no current fulfilment.

For more help with these concepts, see John Stevens' article earlier in this issue.

To take our example of persecution in chapter 13, the futurist position would see the beast as an antichrist figure who will be revealed during the tribulation just before Jesus returns. The number of the beast is often not explained but it might be assumed that its meaning will become clear when the events depicted are fulfilled.

This view clearly takes seriously that much of Revelation does predict 'end-time' events. However it results in very little application to life today, beyond speculating over the future. My view would be that it doesn't take seriously the calls to endurance and faithfulness in the lives of the first readers.

HISTORICIST

This sees Revelation as a chronology of all history from the first century onwards. The letters to the churches are usually seen as relating to the actual first century churches mentioned – although sometimes these are taken as stages of history themselves. But Rev 4-22 is seen as an historical overview. This means that interpretation involves finding one's own moment in time by deciding which scenes have been fulfilled already. This was very popular amongst many Puritans in the 17th century, one of whom who happily claimed, "We live under the opening of the seventh seal and the blowing of the sixth trumpet." It has to be said that historically this has resulted in many 'revisions' as ongoing history didn't confirm what had been found.

Arthur Dent, *The Ruin of Rome: Or, An Exposition Upon the Whole Revelation* (Glasgow: Napirr and Ehull, 1708), 181.

The persecution by the beasts in chapter 13 is read by most historicists as representing papal Rome who persecuted true believers. The number 666 is sometimes taken to be a reference to the Latin language and so refers to the dominance of the papacy through the use of Latin.

I think this interpretation suffers from the same issue as the futurist – that much of the book becomes irrelevant to the first readers, as well as to us (although historicists have regarded some sections of Revelation as relating to our present experience).To my mind it also simply doesn't seem to work given the structure of Revelation we have argued for above, which presents multiple perspectives on the same events, rather than a longer series of successive events.

IDEALIST

This is also referred to as a symbolic or spiritual approach. It sees Revelation as teaching ongoing truths that do not refer to any one moment in history. There are exceptions to this general rule: the letters are taken to refer to the first century churches mentioned, and the final chapters are describing the new creation to come. But the bulk of the book need not relate to specific events in history; it is symbolism teaching truth, not symbols standing for events.

So the persecution by the beast in chapter 13 teaches us that persecution from Satanically-inspired powers will be ongoing through the church age. The number of the beast does not refer to any specific historical figure but has a symbolic meaning – usually that six is one less than the perfect or divine number seven and so the beast represents pretentions to divinity.

I believe this view has great truth to it. As stated above, one of the purposes of apocalyptic literature is to make specific historic examples generic and applicable beyond themselves. So chapter 13 does teach ongoing truth about persecution. The key question is whether it ever had (or will have) a specific historic embodiment.

SUMMARY

The following diagram may help show the differences between these positions:

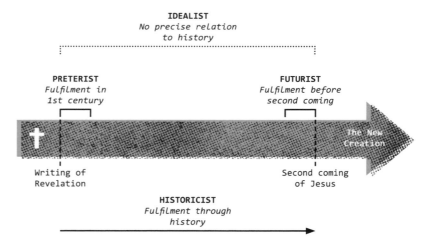

As should be clear, these approaches significantly affect interpretation. Having said that, there are still similarities at many points. So in our example every approach would teach the persecution of God's people from chapter 13, but they would vary in when they placed it and with what level of immediate significance it has to God's people today.

My position is to take the preterist view seriously in looking for first century fulfilment but to take the idealist view in then seeing the general truth being taught which should be applied today. It is worth reading the introductions to different commentaries carefully to see what approach they are taking as that will then underlie subsequent comments on specific passages.

CONSIDER: THE ORIGINAL MEANING AND APPLICATION

Revelation is written to the seven churches in Asia which are listed in chapter 1 (see 1:4, 11) and then in the letters of chapters 2-3. Jesus clearly has a specific message to each of these churches which is given in those letters. We see from them that the churches are in a variety of situations and states of health. Some are staying faithful in persecution, some are tolerating false teaching, and some are close to dying.

However, the recipients of each letter are called to be 'victorious' or to 'conquer'. And of course all get to read the rest of the book which repeats the key idea of 'victory' at significant moments. For example, the book closes with the phrase in 21:7, 'Those who are victorious will inherit all this, and I will be their God and they will be my children'.

Hence a main application of Revelation is to call its original readers to be victorious whatever their starting point is. What being victorious means is then defined by Jesus, who himself 'conquered' by being slain (5:5, 9). So in the crucial middle chapters believers are described as being victorious over Satan in this way:

> **Rev 12:11**
> *They triumphed over him*
> *by the blood of the Lamb*
> *and by the word of their testimony;*
> *they did not love their lives so much*
> *as to shrink from death.*

Triumph comes by faithfulness to the point of death. This connects with another repeated call – that for patient endurance and faithfulness (1:9, 13:10, 14:12).

This picture of triumph through faithfulness clearly applies to those who are persecuted and is a main message of the book. However, the variety of readers depicted in chapters 2-3 means we must be wary of limiting application to persecuted Christians alone. Rather, all of the visions that follow the letters give a picture of reality and of the future that will apply to Christians in varying states, whether persecuted or comfortable. The bottom line is whether we live for this world or for the kingdom to come. Hence all are called to be 'victorious' which means living faithfully for Jesus in every situation.

It should be an obvious point that we must consider what each passage would have meant to the first recipients, and yet the curious world of Revelation can mean we easily forget it in practice. In particular we can read the letters as directed to the seven churches – and so enter into their situation – but then read the visions as being 'abstracted'. Rather we must read the whole book as a whole where the visions have the same overall message and purpose as the letters, and we ask how they would have addressed the seven churches specified.

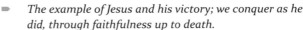

GET HOLD OF THE MAIN MESSAGE

Considering the original readers has laid the foundation for considering the main message of the book. In preaching any biblical book it is helpful to have a summary sentence or catchphrase which captures the overall message. Working hard at these pushes us in our own understanding and then aids coherence and clarity in preaching.

We've just seen the call to victory by way of faithfulness, even in the face of persecution. The reason for such a call is founded on a number of truths:

- ➡ *The example of Jesus and his victory; we conquer as he did, through faithfulness up to death.*

- ➡ *God remains the true God and is sovereign; which we must believe even in the experience of suffering (which is why the true nature of reality must be revealed to us).*

- ➡ *What we see here and now is not the end; rather God will intervene in final judgment and salvation.*

- ➡ *It is through the faithful suffering of his people that God will work to draw more people to himself.*

So in the *NIV Proclamation Bible*, Greg Beale summarises the message of Revelation in this way:

> *Willingness to suffer for faith in, and worship of the sovereign God in his Christ is the path to ultimate victory and the triune God's glory in the new creation.*

I have used the following (based on 1:9):

> *Jesus is king, his kingdom will come, so be patient and stay faithful.*

As one teaches each section of the book, relating it to this overall message is very helpful. So for example in some of the trickier sections, such as chapter 9, one can say that the key issue is whether people will have Satan as their king or will recognise God as the true God and turn back to him. Similarly in the more straightforward sections, such as chapter 22, we must not only describe the new creation to come, but call people to patience and faithfulness now because of it.

NEXT STEPS

So you're interested in preaching through Revelation – what do you do next? I would suggest some study time looking at the sort of material you won't read when preparing a sermon. The introductions to commentaries usually cover the sort of material in this article in greater depth. Also the 'thematic books' section below suggests some books which cover similar material. Study time on these should increase your awareness of the content of the book, its themes, and its structure.

Then consider how you want to divide it up for preaching. Preaching longer sections will mean there's less sense of wading through the same material time after time but will be harder work to prepare. Overall I'd advise taking longer rather than shorter sections in chapters 4-16. Do look at how other preachers have divided it up.

Choose a couple of commentaries (see *PrimerHQ.com* for some suggestions). I would recommend a detailed one such as Beale and an easier to read, more applied one, such as Wilcock or Barnett. You might dip into others for ideas but I found I didn't have time for much more.

Consider a first sermon which opens up the contents of the book. I've preached on 1:1-3 setting the scene, discussing the type of literature, and encouraging us in the blessing we will gain. Of course preach through the seven letters but announce the intention to preach the whole book, and as you go through the letters you should be familiar enough with the whole book to make some reference to what is coming at suitable moments.

Then get preaching.

CONCLUSION

I'm very glad I preached all the way through Revelation. Some of it was the hardest study I've done, and on more than one occasion I admitted my limited understanding to the congregation. But our minds were stretched, our imaginations sparked, and our hearts strengthened. We saw the realities of this world differently; we saw the significance of faithfulness in suffering now; and we looked forward to the day the 'kingdom of this world' becomes 'the kingdom of our Lord and of his Messiah, and he will reign forever' (11:15).

There was far less practical application compared to other New Testament letters. But there was a deep formativeness about it, a shaping of how we looked at the world and what we lived for. As the opening verses promised:

Rev 1:3
> *Blessed is the one who reads aloud the words of this prophecy, and blessed are those who hear it and take to heart what is written in it, because the time is near.*

As our culture becomes increasingly dismissive and antagonistic to the gospel and so to Christians, this may become an increasingly needed vision for us to see. P

Visit *PrimerHQ.com* for recommended reading relating to this article, as well as questions for further thought and discussion relating to each article in this issue.